INSTRUCTOR'S RESOURCE MANUAL

FOR

TEACHING STRATEGIES: A GUIDE TO BETTER INSTRUCTION

3rd Edition

by

Cindee L. Rada
Donald C. Orlich
Robert J. Harder
Washington State University

Donald P. Kauchak
University of Utah

R. A. Pendergrass
Bakersfield, MO Schools

Richard C. Callahan
Shipley Associates

Harry Gibson
St. Martin's College

D. C. Heath and Company

Lexington, Massachusetts   Toronto

USING THE INSTRUCTOR'S MANUAL

Introduction

This manual is designed to help the busy instructor to structure a course around <u>Teaching Strategies: A Guide to Better Instruction</u>, 3rd edition. For each chapter we use a five step sequence in presenting materials for your use and adaptation.

Section 1 lists a short rationale and overview for the chapter. You might edit it for your own syllabus.

Section 2 illustrates two activities that students could complete as meaningful extensions or applications of the topics being developed in the chapter.

Section 3 suggests four recent and annotated references. These papers could be assigned to your students as additional reading, thus expanding treatment in the book.

Section 4 provides a set of objective test items for your use when preparing summative examinations.

Section 5 lists a set of overhead transparency masters that can be used for instruction. The masters are all assembled by chapter at the end of this guide.

Our goal was to meet the many requests for a useable and novel instructor's manual. We tried to prepare a practical one and a guide that reflects how we teach our own methods courses. Please send us your comments or feedback on this addition to the basic textbook.

Acknowledgments

Two individuals provided substantial assistance in preparation of the Manual. Sandra Tyacke prepared the many drafts and the final camera-ready copy. David Coffland modified and prepared the sets of overhead projector transparency masters. We thank our students for their patience as this Manual was assembled.

CONTENTS

CHAPTER 1

TEACHING AS DECISION-MAKING

Overview

Chapter 1 orients the reader to selected aspects of the teachers' world of work. We have found that most preservice (and many inservice) teachers have not seriously analyzed how and why they teach as they do. By providing a brief introduction about decision-making, the school cultures, and pluralistic conflicts, one becomes more aware that there really is no "one best way." Small group discussions on how to develop a teaching framework help students to think through the process.

We suggest briefly analyzing The Nation at Risk and other major reports that have become the cottage industry of school reformers. Point out the simplistic approaches and "one best system" approaches of the majority of the writers. The issues surrounding instructional methods can be used as a summarizing point.

Student Activities

1. Provide the class with references to the many reform papers, reports, and books. Subdivide the class into working and cooperative teams to analyze the major recommendations of selected reports. When discussing teaching education reform be certain to urge the groups to compare the amount of time that would be required to graduate with a teaching certificate now and under the Holmes or Carnegie plans. The students should compute the amount of money needed, but not discussed, by the reformers, and how much they would lose in lost salaries by remaining in school longer. Compare state certification requirements for your state and observe what differences would be needed to teach in your own state if the additional requirements were enforced.

2. If your teacher education program requires direct school experiences while the students enroll in the methods course, then activity two is relevant. Establish a short interview schedule for students in various disciplines or teaching fields. Have the students interview their cooperating teachers to determine what kinds of decisions are made by the teacher, the principal, the staff collectively, or the school district. A grid could be constructed for the class as a means of sharing information.

1

Annotated References for Student Study

    1. Flinders, David J. (1989, May). "Does the 'Art of Teaching' Have a Future?" Educational Leadership, 46(8), 16-20.
    This short piece helps both prospective and practicing secondary teachers to appreciate the subtle and learnable elements of teaching with artistry. The elements of communication, perception, cooperation, and appreciation form a cluster of concepts that are easily applied in classrooms and that extend on treatment.

    2. Pallas, Aaron M., Natriello, Gary, and McDill, Edward L. (1989, June-July). "The Changing Nature of the Disadvantaged Population: Current Dimensions and Future Trends." Educational Researcher, 18(5), 16-22.
    These authors examine the current state of the educationally disadvantaged school population in the United States. Projections for the future are calculated and implications for instruction are stated. Provided here is a data base about a major problem for school teachers--how to work with disadvantaged or at-risk students, as there are so many.

    3. Reilly, David H. (1989, May-June). "A Knowledge Base for Education: Cognitive Science." Journal of Teacher Education, 40(3), 9-13.
    The need for a knowledge base for teacher education students is presented. Reilly stresses the need to develop teaching strategies based on understanding how children or adolescents learn various subjects or fields. Reilly concludes with a call for providing a wide range of teaching skills and processes. These techniques would then be examined in specific instructional contexts. This paper expands our short treatment on the topic.

    4. Spector, Barbara S. (1989, September). "About Stages of Professional Development." Science and Children, 27(1), 62-65.
    While stressing the teaching of science, Spector provides a general five-stage model to describe teacher development. Preservice teachers will especially be interested in Stages I (induction) and II (adjustment). The final three stages will be of interest to inservice teachers--maturation, mid-career crisis, and leadership. The paper provides an effective means for illustrating the normative problems faced by most new teachers and the need for life-long learning. Spector provides a framework that can accompany our discussion on the school culture.

Chapter 1 Test Questions

1. A teacher teaches "intuitively," developing lessons on the basis of feeling for the class. This teacher is using the
   a. artistic approach.
   b. rational planning.
   c. essentialist based curriculum.
   d. none of the above is correct.

2. Intuition as a sole guide to instruction represents a very creative approach for the teaching process.
   a. True
   b. False

3. By 1984, many states across the nation:
   a. passed laws based on clearly written philosophical statements.
   b. mandated accountability testing.
   c. utilized test results to coordinate state objectives regarding instruction.
   d. utilized testing to validate experiential learning programs.

4. Implicit values of a school are reflected in:
   a. extrinsic student awards.
   b. negotiated student-teacher interactions.
   c. the ethos of individual schools.
   d. all of the above.

5. Research-based teaching is interesting, but of little practical value.
   a. True
   b. False

6. Effective schools demonstrate high expectations, but do not test to determine student achievement.
   a. True
   b. False

7. To be "intentionally disinviting" reflects:
   a. planning, compassion and understanding.
   b. teachers who have strong pro-student ideals.
   c. a philosophy of the student as a incompetent person in an impersonal environment.
   d. a teacher who really wants children to learn.

8. "Intentionally inviting" is the desired state for which a teacher should strive.
   a. True
   b. False

9. Some evidence has been found that teachers treat low achievers in the following manner:
   a. criticize low achievers often.
   b. calling on low achievers with greater patience.
   c. providing more wait-time for low achievers.
   d. all of the above.

10. The text states that the most-used teacher activity at the senior high
    school level is:
    a. work on problem solving.
    b. complex learning skills.
    c. lecture and recitations.
    d. no correct answer listed.

11. The "Nation at Risk" report of 1983 and the 1893 report of the Committee
    of Ten agree on all but one point below.
    a. The use of many public school teachers on the national committees.
    b. Academic goals as a drawing force in the high school.
    c. Reforms at a national level.
    d. The importance of high school in our culture.

12. James B. Conant called for educational reform based on:
    a. a site-based approach.
    b. a national curriculum movement.
    c. voucher funding.
    d. different schools for the non-college bound.

13. Social pluralism tends to result in:
    a. homogeneity of goals.
    b. precisely stated goals.
    c. eclectic and ambiguous goals.
    d. all goals being equal.

14. Well-planned teaching strategies are not necessary as teaching is so
    imprecise that any method works as well as another.
    a. True
    b. False

15. The importance of the effective schools research is that it demonstrates:
    a. one best system of instruction exists.
    b. culture and ethos are combined.
    c. that educationally speaking, "the best will survive."
    d. schools are effective when certain elements exist.

16. The basic idea proposed by James Conant in his famous report was that the
    American comprehensive high school:
    a. was in need of total revision.
    b. should be replaced by an entirely new institution.
    c. simply needed "tuning up."
    d. should be redesigned to look like its Russian counterpart.

17. The actual implementation of an educational goal takes place in:
    a. society.
    b. a teacher's classroom.
    c. the deliberations of a school board.
    d. the state legislature.

18. The unit of government that has the most control over public schools in the USA is:
    a. state legislature.
    b. regional cooperative.
    c. the U.S. Department of Education.
    d. The U.S. Supreme Court.
19. James Coleman and Christopher Jencks suggest that one factor is the most important in student achievement:
    a. the curriculum being studied.
    b. individual socio-economic status.
    c. rich instructional methods.
    d. classroom environments.
20. One basic purpose of formative evaluation is to provide students with:
    a. a grade on a report card.
    b. feedback about their learning.
    c. a final grade on a project.
    d. an indication of their relative standing within the group.
21. Middle school/junior high teachers should particularly consider:
    a. the range of students' cognitive levels.
    b. the need for lectures that stress academic excellence.
    c. the use of lectures as a learning aid.
    d. the implementation of corporal punishment.
22. There is some evidence that over several years:
    a. classroom instruction has remained rather stable.
    b. most teachers have become more sensitive to needs of their learners.
    c. the modern high school stresses life adjustment.
    d. high school teachers use more instructional strategies than any other group of teachers.
23. One factor below is not usually cited when discussing effective schools.
    a. Leadership
    b. Curriculum
    c. Cost
    d. School Environment
24. In general, the school culture is:
    a. legislated state by state.
    b. very similar nationally.
    c. dependent on local norms and values.
    d. almost identical to that found in the business sector.
25. As a group, new teachers tend to:
    a. act as change agents in a school.
    b. resist a subject-centered approach to teaching.
    c. feel very secure.
    d. conform to the image of teachers as an authority.

Answer Sheet for Chapter 1

1.	d	13.	c
2.	b	14.	b
3.	b	15.	d
4.	d	16.	c
5.	b	17.	b
6.	b	18.	a
7.	c	19.	b
8.	a	20.	b
9.	a	21.	a
10.	c	22.	a
11.	a	23.	c
12.	a	24.	c
		25.	d

Overhead Transparency Masters for Chapter 1

The following transparency masters are included at the end of the Manual to assist you in presenting concepts from Chapter 1.

1-1.   Teacher as Decision-Maker
1-2.   Understanding School Culture
1-3.   Incentives and School Culture
1-4.   Inviting Student Success
1-5.   Effective Schools
1-6.   Effective Schools
1-7.   Emerging Instructional Issues

CHAPTER 2

DECIDING ON OBJECTIVES

Overview

Chapter 2 provides the initial foundation for planning processes that span through Chapter 5. We stress the use of performance objectives only because so many programs, textbooks, state curriculum guides, and local school district guides require them. Use of performance objectives in the pure form as presented may not actually exist. As computer-aided instruction becomes more useful, teachers will have to prepare performance objectives to maximize student time and learning.

Our integration of PL94-142, brain hemisphericity, and curriculum alignment into this chapter was done with the rationale that each of these facets are, in fact, a part of the teacher's initial planning. Encourage your students to prepare objectives that will stimulate the right brain hemisphere. Further, the notion of curriculum alignment is popularized by Fenwick W. English and others who advocate a wave of "returned accountability." If you infer that we might just be most skeptical about performance objectives making a significant impact on learning, then our subtle implications have been properly interpreted.

Student Activities

1. Obtain a set of your state department of education's curriculum guides. Then, ask your students to identify the kinds of goals and objectives being stressed. If specific student outcomes or performances are specified, have the students classify them as being right or left brain hemisphere oriented. Similarly, analyze the same set of materials seeking evidence of curriculum alignment. Finally, determine the percentage of objectives written with three parts: condition, performance, criterion measure.

2. Each student examines a textbook that is being used in the schools, grades K-12. Examine the teachers' guides to observe the kind of performance objectives supplied by publishing companies. After you study Chapter 4 about the taxonomies, repeat Activity 2, but categorize the objectives via the six levels of the cognitive taxonomy.

Annotated References for Student Study

1. English, Fenwick W. (1986-1987, December-January). "It's Time to Abolish Conventional Curriculum Guides." Educational Leadership, 44(4), 50-52.
    An advocate for curriculum alignment provides five logical criticisms of typical curriculum guides. English then establishes a framework for matching content, objectives, assignments, and tests. Although he presents a simplified version of the alignment process, novices will benefit from this one, albeit biased point of view.

2. Fountain, Juanita Cummings and H. Thompson Fillmer. (1987, Winter). "Hemispheric Brain Preference: What are the Educational Implications?" Reading Improvement, 24(4), 252-255.
    The authors discuss the relationship between brain hemispheric preferences from a study of selected fourth and seventh graders. Using appropriate instruments, Fountain and Fillmer provide three basic preferences--left, integrated, and right. Schools tend to stress left functions over right ones. However, in this study the integrated preference tended to be more commonplace. While the experimental data are not conclusive, the authors conclude that cerebral hemispheric functions affect learning. They strongly endorse having teachers provide experiences that enable integration of brain processes.

3. Melnick, Steven A. and Robert K. Gable. (1989, February). "High School Curriculum Alignment: Much Work to be Done." The Clearing House, 62(6), 245-249.
    This study makes a nice companion piece to English's paper. Melnick and Gable briefly discuss curriculum alignment and then present survey data from Connecticut educators relating to the concept.
    Data show that teachers carefully plan for instruction, including the preparation of stated objectives. However, it appeared that in Connecticut teachers selectively taught content not typically covered on standardized tests: Or, all that work and little alignment.

4. Oliva, Peter F. (1988). "Curriculum Goals and Objectives," In Developing the Curriculum. Glenview, Ill.: Scott Foresman and Company, Chapter 8, 258-288.
    Oliva presents a detailed explanation about the relationships of goals and aims to curriculum and instructional objectives. Specific examples are provided from school district documents. Examination of Table 8-1 shows how careful planning is needed when one translates major goals into performance-based objectives.

Chapter 2 Test Questions

1. Instructional priorities are most directly affected by:
   a. the U.S. Congress.
   b. college professors.
   c. teachers.
   d. all of the above equally.

2. An objective that stresses experiences of observation would be classified as:
   a. performance.
   b. process.
   c. content.
   d. behavioral.

3. Interpretation of the term "least restrictive environment" would mean:
   a. mainstreaming of handicapped children would be one option.
   b. mainstreaming of handicapped children would be the only option.
   c. handicapped children must be kept at home.
   d. a parent may request any educational treatment for a handicapped child.

4. The term "least restrictive environment" would be found in:
   a. National Defense Education Act (NDEA).
   b. Elementary and Secondary Education Act (ESEA).
   c. John Dewey's writings.
   d. Public Law 94-142.

5. Pygmalion in the classroom seems to demonstrate that:
   a. "late bloomers" can be readily identified.
   b. students usually achieve what their teachers expect them to.
   c. teacher behavior is always controlled by students.
   d. there is no relationship between teacher expectations and student achievement.

6. Performance objectives help to clarify instruction for:
   a. students as they study.
   b. teachers as they plan for instruction.
   c. items a and b are both correct.
   d. none of the above is correct.

7. Which is the most accurate assessment of the performance objective movement?
   a. The emphasis is on student outputs.
   b. The emphasis is on what the teacher does (inputs).
   c. There is no evidence to show that they work under educational conditions.
   d. It is an "anti-accountability technique.

8. A teacher who uses performance objectives correctly will:
    a. assign only A and B grades.
    b. use only satisfactory and unsatisfactory in grading.
    c. establish grading criteria.
    d. will not assign grades at all.
9. The authors would view performance objectives as:
    a. an absolute educational necessity.
    b. one technique by which to specify instruction.
    c. the only technique that a teacher may use.
    d. quite really, a big waste of teacher's time.
10. Which item is not a part of a performance objective?
    a. Criterion.
    b. Performance.
    c. Condition.
    d. Rationale.
11. Curriculum alignment refers to:
    a. assessment, instruction, observations.
    b. goals, the society, and the culture.
    c. assessment, values, observations.
    d. performance objectives, assignments, and tests.
12. To align the curriculum in part means to:
    a. file performance objectives.
    b. explicitly test what is explicitly taught.
    c. compare standardized tests with other schools nationally.
    d. test students on every possible learning objective.
13. Learning is defined as a change in the learner's:
    a. behavior.
    b. attitude toward classmates.
    c. use of study skills.
    d. attendance.
14. Hemisphericity as applied to educational planning means that the:
    a. teacher must determine which brain hemisphere each student uses to complete school work.
    b. students must determine whether to use the left, right, or the whole brain when doing school work.
    c. teachers tend to over-stress right brain hemisphere functions.
    d. teachers tend to over-stress left brain hemisphere functions.
15. The concept of brain hemisphericity is:
    a. one means of accounting for specific types of learning.
    b. untested and is just more educational theory.
    c. impossible to use in any meaningful way in the public schools.
    d. written into the PL 94-142 legislation.

16. An "Individualized Educational Plan" is a major component of:
    a. curriculum alignment.
    b. the behavioral approach to learning.
    c. mainstreaming selected students.
    d. applying brain hemisphericity.

Below are nine paired statements, i.e., 17a and 17b. For each pair, mark your answer for the objective which best meets the requirements for a performance objective.

17. a. Develop one roll of black and white film.
    b. Understand how a developing agent works.
18. a. Select six useful objectives.
    b. Know what makes six objectives useful.
19. a. Select from alternatives those definitions which best define the terms.
    b. Know all the meanings of the terms.
20. a. Solve ten math problems requiring an understanding of place value.
    b. Solve ten math problems having two place values.
21. a. After watching the movie "Teacher."
    b. Using your notebook.
22. a. Grasp the important people in the news.
    b. Match the names of people in the news with their pictures.
23. a. Select three good poems from good and bad examples.
    b. Evaluate a set of six poems by using the criteria checklist.
24. a. Classify the leaf collection into four major groups.
    b. Infer from the story the main theme.
25. a. Complete with accuracy the 10 problems.
    b. Correctly completing 8 of the 10 examples.

Answer Sheet for Chapter 2

1.	c	14.	d
2.	b	15.	a
3.	a	16.	c
4.	d	17.	a
5.	b	18.	a
6.	c	19.	a
7.	a	20.	b
8.	c	21.	b
9.	b	22.	b
10.	d	23.	b
11.	d	24.	a
12.	b	25.	b
13.	a		

Overhead Transparency Masters for Chapter 2

The following transparency masters are included at the end of the Manual to assist you in presenting concepts from Chapter 2.

2-1. Goals
2-2. Objectives
2-3. Performance Objectives
2-4. Rationale for Performance Objectives
2-5. Problems with Performance Objectives
2-6. Left Hemispheric Functions
2-7. Left Hemispheric Functions
2-8. Right Hemispheric Functions
2-9. Right Hemispheric Functions
2-10. Curriculum Alignment

CHAPTER 3

DECISIONS ABOUT SEQUENCING INSTRUCTION

Overview

Chapter 3 presents the reader with four major models for organizing
lessons or units of instruction. Beginning teachers tend not to organize
concepts, generalizations or principles that are embodied in a discipline or
subject area into an integrated whole. Thus, it is important for them to
understand that there are several approaches that have been successfully used
to accomplish that planning. The models presented in this chapter are only
illustrative of an array of models available to teachers. The Concept Attainment Model is primarily cognitive while another model, Diagnostic Prescriptive, is problem centered. The Task Analysis Model tends to be linear and
sequential whereas the Advance Organizer Model, if all components are used, is
very interactive as is the Concept Analysis Model. Common features of all of
the models stress that meaningful learning is subdivided into parts. In that
manner the intended information can be understood and is sequenced so that the
parts contribute to understanding of a body of knowledge. Each of the models
aids understanding in a different way.

It is suggested that students have an experience with each of the
models in this chapter. It is important to analyze each experience so that
students understand the common lesson planning principles embedded in each
model. Further, students must understand the unique features of each model.
A chart describing common and unique lesson planning characteristics of each
model provides an excellent chapter summary activity. Following are several
activities that the authors have found to be successful.

Student Activities

1. For a Task Analysis activity, divide the class in subject area
groups. Each group will decide on a single lesson performance objective. Have
each small group prepare a task analysis of the objective, recording the
results on an overhead transparency. Have the group present their work to the
class. After several presentations, discuss advantages and problems of task
analysis.

2. Have each student develop a lesson plan and demonstrate the Concept Attainment Model with the Advance Organizer Model. Depending on the size of the class, you can either have each student present a micro lesson or divide the class so that one-half present the Concept Attainment Model and one-half the Advance Organizer Model. Discuss content appropriate for each model.

3. For the Diagnostic-Prescriptive Model, the case study approach has worked well. For optimum results, use several different case studies ranging from crisis problems to normal class learning situations. Divide the class into groups of 4 to 5 students to develop a Diagnostic-Prescriptive lesson. Have students share their lessons in class.

If you should have a practicum or observation component for the course, then ask students to use one of the models or have them identify lessons for which one of the models is appropriate.

Annotated References for Student Study

1. Mitman, Alexis L., John R. Mergendollar, Virginia A. Marchman, and Martin J. Packer. (1987, Winter). "Instruction Addressing the Components of Scientific Literacy and Its Relations to Student Outcomes." American Educational Research Journal, 24(4), 611-633.

Using ethnographic techniques, data were gathered from 11 seventh grade teachers of life science. Seldom, if ever, did the cohort group make any connection between the science content and its societal, reasoning, historical, or attitudinal implications. In short, context was omitted from science content. This study is useful in showing how a hierarchy chart or set of independent sequences could be made by the teacher to insure coverage and review of contextual elements of instruction.

2. Townsend, Michael A. R. and Anne Clarihen. (1989). Journal of Reading Behavior, 21(1), 15-35.

The authors present results of their research study on 8-year-old children. In one case, the verbal advance organizer helped the comprehension on only those children who had strong prior knowledge. However, a second experiment was done where pictures were added to the advance organizer. This technique facilitated comprehension of children who had weaker prior knowledge. This study illustrates the need for various modes of advance organizers.

3. Washington, Valerie M. (1988, Summer). "Report Writing: A Practical Application of Semantic Mapping." The Teacher Educator, 24(1), 24-30.

While this case study illustrates semantic mapping (discussed in Chapter 6), the structure of the use is a classic example of combining advance

organizers with task analysis. Each specific teaching task is illustrated
with several examples.

4. Martin, Barbara L. (1989, August). "A Checklist for Designing
Instruction in the Affective Domain." Educational Technology, 29(8), 7-15.

In one paper, Martin very appropriately illustrates concepts of
sequencing, task analysis, and use of hierarchies. The Affective Domain is
often neglected from lesson considerations. This paper provides a detailed
application of how to design lessons for affective instruction by using the
tools we present in Chapter 3. Further, Martin's paper would be an ideal
discussion piece when you assign Chapter 4--The Taxonomies.

Chapter 3 Test Questions

1. Task analysis reflects which assumption?
   a. Communicating to students what is to be taught is unimportant.
   b. Learning is somewhat random in the schools, thus, it helps to add a sequence.
   c. The schools must help students to appreciate our culture in the best possible manner.
   d. Teaching tasks sequentially has been and continues to be critical in creating student success.

2. Which statement is <u>not</u> valid when discussing task analysis?
   a. Learning is more manageable.
   b. Learning is more meaningful.
   c. The process illustrates a relationship between various concepts.
   d. None of the above is invalid.

3. Which is the lowest level objective in a task analysis?
   a. Mastery.
   b. Terminal objectives.
   c. Entry level skills.
   d. All of these are equal in value.

4. Which statement is most valid?
   a. Dependent sequences are less crucial than independent sequences when diagnosing difficulties.
   b. It is not possible to sequence material dependently to make a learning prescription.
   c. When student difficulty is diagnosed, dependent sequencing is especially useful in deriving a prescription to improve learning.
   d. When student difficulty is diagnosed, sequencing is then done by the student.

5. Which set of action verbs would imply the simplest set of learning objectives if you were using task analysis?
   a. Interpret, illustrate, judge, solve.
   b. Define, record, cite, identify.
   c. List, compile, solve, explain.
   d. Estimate, contrast, judge, rate.

6. Advance organizers provide for:
   a. six-step interaction models.
   b. "ideational scaffolds."
   c. concept sequencing.
   d. terminal objectives.

7. Using the concept analysis model requires a careful selection of:
   a. the intermediate objectives.
   b. the values to be taught.
   c. the content to be used.
   d. the test items.

8. The Ausubel Model is most nearly an example of:
    a. deductive presentations.
    b. mastery learning.
    c. inductive presentations.
    d. hypothetic-deductive presentations.
9. The Ausubel Model begins with which phase?
    a. Progressive differentiation.
    b. Advance organizer.
    c. Integrative reconciliation.
    d. Monitoring and adjusting.
10. In the Ausubel Model, progressive differentiation is:
    a. the closure of the lesson.
    b. a subdivision of the lesson into more complex parts.
    c. a focusing event.
    d. the comparing and contrasting of components.
11. For an Ausubel lesson to work efficiently, the teacher's advance organizer should provide students with:
    a. an understandable focus.
    b. a visual representation of the relationship.
    c. examples to explain the concept or analysis.
    d. all of the above.

True or False: Place a "T" for true or an "F" for False on your answer sheet.

12. Isolating what is to be taught helps makes learning more manageable.
13. When an instructor utilizes a hierarchical level of analysis, then students will be more likely to learn more complex content.
14. In a properly structured learning hierarchy model, the end result will be the terminal objective.
15. In practice, when you use a task analysis, you define separate tasks before ordering them.
16. The basic reason for evaluation in the diagnostic prescription model is to make the final grade for that unit or subject.
17. In general, it makes little difference how or when a teacher introduces items arranged in a dependent sequence.
18. Using a hierarchy chart such as Gagne's requires the students to sequence the way they complete the assignment.
19. While there is much theory about advance organizers and hierarchy charts, in reality no curriculum or published program has ever used them.
20. The diagnostic-prescription model is only used with handicapped children.

Answer Sheet for Chapter 3

1.	d	11.	d
2.	d	12.	T
3.	c	13.	T
4.	c	14.	T
5.	a	15.	T
6.	b	16.	F
7.	c	17.	F
8.	a	18.	F
9.	b	19.	F
10.	b	20.	F

Overhead Transparency Masters for Chapter 3

The following transparency masters are included at the end of the Manual to assist you in presenting concepts from Chapter 3.

3-1. Models of Lesson Organization
3-2. Task Analysis
3-3. Concept Analysis
3-4. Advance Organizer
3-5. Diagnostic Prescriptive

CHAPTER 4

DECIDING ON LEVELS OF INSTRUCTION: INTRODUCING THE TAXONOMIES

Overview

In this chapter we introduce the reader to taxonomies as conceptual tools to analyze teaching. Three taxonomies are introduced: (1) the cognitive domain deals with knowledge and thinking skills, (2) the affective domain deals with attitudes and values, and (3) the psychomotor domain focuses on the development of physical strength and coordination.

The taxonomies are useful analytical tools to help teachers think about the range of existing goals in the school curriculum. They also help in the decision-making process of selecting an appropriate strategy to reach an educational objective. Stress the point that a knowledge of the taxonomies is an essential part of a professional teacher's knowledge base. Provide opportunities for students to apply the taxonomies in their own content areas and at appropriate grade levels.

Student Activities

1. Divide the class into groups on the basis of content area or grade level. Have each group write one objective in a given content area for each of the six levels of Bloom's Taxonomy. Share these with the other groups and discuss:

    a. problems encountered in writing objectives at different levels.
    b. possible teaching strategies to use in reaching each objective.
    c. ways of evaluating learning at each level.

2. To reinforce application to the real world, bring in to class one or more of the following instructional materials:

    a. student textbook,
    b. teacher edition of a text,
    c. state or district curriculum guides,
    d. test or quiz used in the schools.

Analyze these in class in terms of the taxonomies by having students classify objectives or questions by domain and level. Compare your results with research discussed in the chapter.

Annotated References for Student Study

1. Beyer, Barry K. (1984, April) Improving Thinking Skills-- Practical Approaches. Phi Delta Kappan, 41, 556-560.
    This excellent and readable article explains how Bloom's Taxonomy relates to the larger area of thinking skills. The article describes the six levels of the Taxonomy as "micro thinking"™ skills, basic and discrete processes that serve as building blocks for larger processes like problem solving and inquiry. Beyer also discusses issues involved in teaching thinking skills.

2. Nickerson, Raymond S. (1985, February) Understanding, Under- standing. American Journal of Education, 93(2), 201-237.
    This review article analyzes the process of understanding from a psychological perspective. It argues persuasively that understanding is a complex, multi-level phenomena that requires skillful teaching. The writer also discusses issues in the assessment of student understanding. We view this paper as absolutely must reading!

3. Prawat, R. (1989, Spring) Promoting Access to Knowledge, Strategy and Disposition in Students: A Research Synthesis. Review of Educational Research, 59(1), 1-41.
    This review of the literature explores information storage and retrieval from an information processing perspective. It argues that students' ability to access information stored in memory is influenced by how the information is stored and students' awareness of the organization of the storage system. While more theoretical, Prawat does an excellent job of describing current thinking on cognitive functions.

4. Shuell, Thomas J. (1986, Winter) Cognitive Conceptions of Learning. Review of Educational Research, 56(4), 411-436.
    Shuell does an excellent job of describing the differences between cognitive and behavioral views of learning. In doing so he discusses a number of topics central to the taxonomies: the critical need of active learning; the central importance of understanding; and, the cumulative nature of learning. Students with a background in educational psychology will find this a useful synthesis of recent research on learning and thinking.

Chapter 4 Test Questions

Part I--Taxonomies: Classify each of the following by using the code below for the Domain.

A = Affective   C = Cognitive   P = Psychomotor

1. After watching a videotape rerun of a two-minute dance routine, students will perform the dance movement correctly.

2. Students will show their appreciation of the privileges of American citizenship by continuing to vote in elections over the following five years.

3. Given ten audio examples of music, the students will categorize the types of music played with 80% accuracy.

4. Students will develop an appreciation for good hygiene habits, so that they will wash their hands with soap and water before preparing a meal.

5. Given a demonstration dummy, the student will demonstrate correct CPR technique on both an infant and on an adult.

6. At home, the student will demonstrate good study habits by making a schedule of assignments, and setting aside a study time nightly.

7. Following the pattern, the student will correctly cut out the material without error.

8. To show their appreciation for safety, students will demonstrate good safety practices during physical education class activities.

9. Given a map of Europe, the student will be able to identify those countries overtaken by Nazi Germany during World War II without error.

10. In classroom situations, students will monitor their own honesty by doing their own work on assignments and tests.

Part II--Cognitive Domain: Categorize the following objective and questions using the following key.

K = Knowledge;   C = Comprehensive;   Ap = Application   An = Analysis
S = Synthesis; and E = Evaluation

11. Given a new problem, the student will correctly solve the equation without error.

12. For the high school retail marketing student to recognize balance in a merchandising display so that the student will, when given ten pictures of ten different displays, point out the six that are balanced.

13. After reading the two novels, the student will write a three-page paper comparing the idea of "heroes" as viewed in both novels.

14. Given a list of ten definitions and terms, the student will correctly match the terms to the definitions.

15. Given a simple article from a newspaper, the student will summarize the article including at least three of the major points.

16. Twelfth-grade art students should define the concept of creativity in their own minds so that, when given the question, Are all artists creative? the student will write a five-page paper stating their opinions, using at least five examples.

17. Given examples of Impressionist and non-Impressionist paintings, the student will be able to correctly identify those examples which are Impressionist.

18. For fifth-grade science students to understand how to utilize the scientific method so that, from memory, the students will list its steps without error.

19. When given the power of the generator to the closest watt, electrical engineering students will know how to determine generator wattage.

20. Given $100 to spend, the student will plan a menu for a family of four for an entire week, including the four basic food groups recommended daily.

21. The advanced music composition student will understand what constitutes a musical composition so that, when given paper, pencil, and access to a piano, the student can compose an original musical composition, including melody and harmony, of at least six measures.

22. Given a map of the United States, the student will label the Thirteen Original Colonies with fewer than three errors.

23. Given ten sentences, the student will be able to identify correctly by underlining the verb in each sentence.

24. For fourth-grade mathematics students to understand how to solve a two-step problem so that, when given five new word problems, they will follow proper procedures without further instructions to solve the problems. Criteria for evaluation will be both using at least two steps to solve the problems as well as determining the correct answer.

25. Given an actual malfunctioning automobile engine, the auto mechanics student will diagnose the problem, explaining the causes of the malfunction.

Answer Sheet for Chapter 4

Part I   Part II

1. Psychomotor   11. Application
2. Affective   12. Comprehension
3. Cognitive   13. Analysis
4. Affective   14. Knowledge
5. Psychomotor   15. Comprehension
6. Affective   16. Evaluation
7. Psychomotor   17. Comprehension
8. Affective   18. Knowledge
9. Cognitive   19. Application
10. Affective   20. Application
                                       21. Synthesis
                                       22. Knowledge
                                       23. Comprehension
                                       24. Application
                                       25. Analysis

Overhead Transparency Masters for Chapter 4

        The following transparency masters are included at the end of the
Manual to assist you in presenting concepts from Chapter 4.

4-1. Cognitive Taxonomy
4-2. Knowledge
4-3. Comprehension
4-4. Application and Analysis
4-5. Synthesis
4-6. Evaluation
4-7. Affective Domain
4-8. Jewett and Mullan's Taxonomy

CHAPTER 5

DECISIONS ABOUT LESSON PLANNING

Overview

Lesson planning is one of those activities where teachers in the field spend a few seconds per day to sketch an outline or hours to design elaborate models. Our goal is to illustrate a very wide variety of plans using Louis Sullivan's dictum that "form follows function." As we only stress daily planning, it is important for you, the course instructor, to introduce the concept of unit plans and long-range planning. We also suggest reviewing Chapter 2 where the topic of IEPs is introduced.

We recognize that fads abound in the educational enterprise. Some lesson plan designers have vastly over-sold their ideas and we do caution the reader in that regard. Finally, we incorporate micro teaching with this chapter, i.e., have each student prepare a single concept lesson and teach to one objective.

Student Activities

1. After reviewing the parts of a lesson plan, as in Chapter 5 Teaching Strategies, give each student a blank lesson plan format. The assignment is to have students complete the lesson plan for the next class session.

During the next class session, divide the class into their respective content areas. Have each group critique each other's individual lesson plans, making sure all the parts are included.

2. After examining the Kaplan Matrix in Table 5-3 in Teaching Strategies, divide the class into groups of four. Distribute a blank Kaplan Matrix to each group.

The group then decides on a unit of study. They then proceed to complete the matrix. A short group interaction could then take place illustrating how each group completed the activity.

Annotated References for Student Study

1.   Brown, Deborah Sardo. (1988, September). "Twelve Middle-School Teachers' Planning." The Elementary School Journal, 89(1), 69-87.
     A research review illustrating differences between how teachers are taught to plan instruction and how at least some teachers actually do such planning. A provocative article that could serve as a discussion topic for "theoretical versus practical" in instructional planning.

2.   Flouris, George. (1988, January/February). "Teaching About Ancient Greece: A Model Teaching Unit." The Social Studies, 79(1), 25-31.
     The writer illustrates a method for developing short instructional units. Gagne's principles of learning, as noted in Chapter 3, are used to enlarge upon and make more clear the general suggestions in most teacher's editions of a text.

3.   Kanatani, Kim. (1988, March). "Michael Heizer." Art Education, 41(2), 26-27.
     As a regular feature entitled "Instructional Resources: Technology," Art Education offers sample lesson plans to accompany an illustrated art work. Kanatani refers to Michael Heizer's sculpture "Double Negative." The lesson plans provide a useful model as well as a practical link between curricular areas.

4.   Keller, Clair W. (1988, May/June). "Enhancing the Expository Approach for Teaching History." The Social Studies, 79(3), 92-96.
     Asserting that teachers place heavy reliance upon textbooks and a lecture-discussion approach, Keller presents a 5-step planning model to help teachers organize a text into a more useful pattern for a lecture-discussion format.

Chapter 5 Test Questions

1. In lesson planning, the term "unit" best describes:
    a. an outline of how the lesson will be taught.
    b. the name of the larger element of instructions of which the parti-
        cular lesson is part.
    c. a brief justification of why students should learn what is being
        taught.
    d. checklist of everything.

2. In lesson planning, the term "instructional goal" best describes:
    a. an outline or description of what is to be taught.
    b. a description of what the students will be able to do as a conse-
        quence of the lesson.
    c. an outline of how the lesson will be taught.
    d. post-instruction assessment of student performance.

3. In lesson planning, the term "rationale" best describes:
    a. a brief justification of why students should learn what is being
        taught.
    b. a description of what students will be able to do as a consequence of
        the lesson.
    c. an outline of how the lesson will be taught.
    d. an outcome students are to achieve on completion of the total unit of
        instruction.

4. When a teacher reviews the goals, content, and activities of a lesson
    prior to presentation, it is a:
    a. rationale plan.
    b. post analysis of lesson plan.
    c. pre-lesson plan.
    d. content review.

5. When an instructor teaches by the "what am I going to do today?" method,
    it can be described as:
    a. thoughtful planning.
    b. systematic planning.
    c. weak planning.
    d. eclectic planning.

6. Lesson plans have value in that they:
    a. keep the principal off-guard.
    b. articulate the teacher's ideas, activities, and assignments.
    c. assist only beginning teachers.
    d. can be used year after year without modification.

7. Techniques suitable for obtaining information regarding student back-
    ground or entry level include:
    a. observation in hallways.
    b. socio-demographic analysis.
    c. interpersonal interest inventory.
    d. review test scores.

8. Process objectives are used in:
   a. writing performance objectives.
   b. specifying procedural outcomes.
   c. used in behavior modification.
   d. should not be used at all.
9. Monitoring student behavior during the lesson is important because:
   a. the teacher needs to diagnose how well the students are learning.
   b. students need to be kept awake.
   c. part of evaluation is classroom discipline.
   d. none of the above.
10. Direct instruction is most often associated with:
    a. Johnson and Johnson.
    b. Slavin.
    c. Brophy and Good.
    d. Peterson, Engleman, Carnine, and Rosenshine.
11. Micro-teaching allows teaching to occur with:
    a. practice and support.
    b. little or reduced threat.
    c. self-evaluation and feedback.
    d. all of the above.
12. Micro-teaching drawbacks are associated with:
    a. loss of reality.
    b. applies to pre-service teachers only.
    c. not useful to work on skills.
    d. there are no benefits to practicing.
13. Evaluation of teaching on an on-going basis is classified as:
    a. summative.
    b. formative.
    c. subjective.
    d. required.
14. The focusing event in direct instruction is used to:
    a. seek closure.
    b. checking for understanding.
    c. introduce a lesson.
    d. close the lesson.

Mark a "T" for true and an "F" for false.

15. The authors of the text suggest that lesson planning strictly follow one method.
16. All objectives as a lesson plan should be organized and presented in a hierarchical fashion.
17. Including a rationale clarifies the lesson intent.
18. Students drill and practice should be used for keeping the lid on student behavior.
19. Direct instruction is one system that tends to involve all students.
20. Direct instruction is really the Hunter model.

Answer Sheet for Chapter 5

1.	b	11.	d
2.	b	12.	a
3.	a	13.	b
4.	c	14.	c
5.	c	15.	F
6.	b	16.	T
7.	d	17.	T
8.	b	18.	F
9.	a	19.	T
10.	d	20.	T

Overhead Transparency Masters for Chapter 5

The following transparency masters are included at the end of the Manual to assist you in presenting concepts from Chapter 5.

5-1. Lesson-Planning Cycle
5-2. Lesson Implementation
5-3. Lesson Implementation
5-4. Instructional Procedures
5-5. Teacher Effectiveness
5-6. Rosenshine's Effective Teachers
5-7. ITIP Model
5-8. Direct Instruction
5-9. Direct Instruction--Weaknesses
5-10. Direct Instruction Steps

CHAPTER 6

DECIDING HOW TO ASK QUESTIONS

Overview

Chapter 6 illustrates the use of a systematic method of conducting traditional recitation periods. The evidence overwhelmingly favors the "wait time" technique, so that those who want to refute it must provide substantive evidence to the contrary! Our goal is to show how to develop a repertoire of question-asking skills, so that teaching behaviors reflect a consistent and positive approach to verbal interactions.

Our experience has been that this chapter should be followed immediately by a video-taped, micro-teaching experience so that all students can apply selected techniques. We encourage the course instructor to discuss the concept of "equity of classroom participation" so that prospective or in-service teachers realize that all children must be truly treated equally during the classroom recitation periods.

Student Activities

1. Assign students the task of preparing a concept map from one question or area in their respective disciplines or favorite teaching field. After making the map, students can discuss their products in groups of four to six. Encourage each small group to produce a creative interpretation of one of the maps.

2. Ask the students to tabulate a series of questions asked by their college professors. Tabulations should follow a uniform method or code. From the data, students should be able to conclude whether professors ask questions in any systematic patterns and if there is any gender bias during the recitation periods.

This assignment could be used most effectively during student teaching episodes. Results could be compared to the main points of this chapter and, if need be, remedial action taken.

Annotated References for Student Study

1. Dillon, J. T. (1988). "Student Questions," in Questioning and Teaching: A Manual of Practice. New York: Teachers College Press, 6-40 (Chapter 2).
This reference by a world authority on questioning processes provides an excellent rationale for teachers to encourage their own students to ask questions during the classroom recitation periods, rather than the teacher doing the questioning.

2. Swicegood, Philip R. and James L. Parsons. (1989, Spring). "Better Questions and Answers Equal Success." Teaching Exceptional Children, 21(3), 4-8.
The authors illustrate several novel techniques that can enhance student question-asking behaviors. Ten easy to use strategies are provided for use with exceptional children--or, with all pupils.

3. Tobin, Kenneth. (1987, Spring). "The Role of Wait Time in Higher Cognitive Level Learning." Review of Educational Research, 57(1), 69-95.
Although summarized in Chapter 6, we strongly urge the reading of Tobin's detailed and insightful review of questioning, wait time, and student verbal achievement. Perhaps this piece alone convinces even the toughest skeptic of the value of using systematic classroom questioning strategies.

4. Watson, Edward D. (1988, September). "How to Ask Better Questions." Learning, 17(2), 94.
Watson provides an easy to duplicate (with permission of course) set of tips of asking questions. He illustrates four categories: variety, inference, support, and conclusion. The use of these categories and other succinct tips are especially applicable at the elementary or middle school levels.

Chapter 6 Test Questions

1. There is some evidence to indicate that a vast majority of questions in textbooks are at the following cognitive level:
   a. knowledge
   b. comprehension
   c. application
   d. evaluation

2. Which strategy would best aid a teacher in organizing a lesson which entails the use of appropriate questions?
   a. Develop the questions, then state the objectives.
   b. Identify the objectives of the lesson, then develop the questions.
   c. Write a list of questions to be asked prior to the class and use them.
   d. Ask a series of questions that can't be answered by the class, then give them assignments to find the answers.

3. A positive consequence of the Multiple Response questioning is that:
   a. there will be less student participation.
   b. the teacher is more actively involved.
   c. it provides a framework for building student interactions.
   d. None of the above are apparent.

4. Which trend is the most accurate conclusion from several research studies?
   a. Teachers dislike asking questions in their classes.
   b. Most teachers carefully plan their teaching and questioning.
   c. Teachers stress critical thinking skills when questioning.
   d. Teachers tend to use questions which elicit student responses which can be classified as knowledge.

5. The use of a convergent, rapid-fire technique is borrowed from:
   a. Hunter's instructional model.
   b. concept mapping.
   c. wait-time research.
   d. direct instruction.

6. Research since the early 1900s indicates that teachers' questioning practices have tended to be:
   a. limited, as indicated by low numbers of questions daily.
   b. progressive from recall types to highly sophisticated types.
   c. rather consistent.
   d. based on the theory of "cognitive dissidence."

7. Which technique has been identified as helping students to listen more effectively during class discussions?
   a. The teacher should refrain from repeating both students' questions and responses.
   b. The teacher should repeat only the students' responses.
   c. The teacher should always repeat students' questions and responses.
   d. The teacher should always restate the question in at least two different ways.

8. When prompting students to help them reach a correct answer, the teacher should always:
   a. restate the question more loudly.
   b. do the prompting in a positive manner.
   c. first tell the student what is wrong with the answer.
   d. call on someone else to get the answer, then have the first student repeat it.

9. Identify the explanation below which is **NOT** a major reason for exercising pause, or wait-time, when questioning.
   a. It keeps all students "attending" to the question.
   b. It provides time for the students to give a very quick response.
   c. It provides time for the teacher to interpret non-verbal signals.
   d. It gives the students a chance to think.

10. When a student gives an incorrect response, the teacher should:
    a. prompt or probe.
    b. use a multiple response approach.
    c. ask that student to repeat the question.
    d. ignore the response and proceed with lesson, lest the teacher offend the student.

11. One way to encourage non-volunteers to respond during class discussion is to:
    a. ignore the students.
    b. ask the students more difficult questions.
    c. Prepare the students the day before with the questions you may ask in class.
    d. give discussion points for those who participate.

12. Nearly all questioning strategies may be classified into three categories:
    a. rapid-fire, objective, divergent.
    b. cognitive, affective, psychomotor.
    c. convergent, divergent, evaluative.
    d. open-ended, closed, and structured.

13. Students' listening skills will **NOT** improve:
    a. if the students repeat their own responses.
    b. by the students repetition of teacher's questions.
    c. if students are told that you are using a relatively new questioning method.
    d. by the teacher's repetition of student responses.

14. Teachers should:
    a. concentrate on asking a few highly verbal students to respond.
    b. complete student responses for the student who has partially completed a response.
    c. call on only those students who have their hands up.
    d. make sure all students are given time to respond.
15. In general, research about cognitive levels of student responses and higher level teacher questions:
    a. show that a positive relationship exists.
    b. indicate that there is a negative relationship (e.g., high level questions cause low level responses).
    c. substantiate that there is no need to train teachers to ask questions.
    d. indicate that teachers will ask questions how they please even with training.
16. In a lesson plan, you can list words or questions that may be used to prompt students related to a specific question. You cannot prepare all the sequencing for prompting before class begins because:
    a. generally, the right answer will be given.
    b. prompting questions are based on specific student responses.
    c. it takes too long for a teacher to prepare the questions.
    d. students will not respond to prompting.
17. Divergent thinking may be encouraged by:
    a. having several students respond to a single question.
    b. using convergent, rapid-fire questions.
    c. deciding on the correct answers in the lesson plan.
    d. All of the above are correct.
18. The technique for wait-time is to:
    a. call on the student, ask the question, and listen for a response.
    b. ask the question, pause, call on a student.
    c. call on the student, pause, and ask the question.
    d. pause, call on the student, ask the question.
19. Punitive questions is:
    a. an effective teaching strategy.
    b. effective for the slower students.
    c. ineffective and not supported by research.
    d. very effective as shown by numerous research studies.
20. The Suchman technique is an application of:
    a. concept mapping.
    b. evaluative questioning.
    c. using inductive logic.
    d. using deductive logic.

21. One teacher idiosyncrasy to avoid during questioning is:
    a. looking at the student you select to answer a question.
    b. calling on three students to respond to one question.
    c. answering a tough question when a student misses it.
    d. pausing after a student responds to a question.
22. One technique that can be used effectively is to:
    a. allow students to ask questions.
    b. discourage all volunteers.
    c. repeat those questions that are silly.
    d. keep a list of every question that you'll ask.
23. As a teacher, you decide to make a statement about some action or issue. This behavior is:
    a. universally condemned as being opinionated.
    b. effective to elicit student reactions.
    c. one form of a teacher "put down."
    d. not a way to get student responses.
24. You tabulate the number of teacher questions asked during a 25-minute recitation period and note that 40 questions were asked. From these date the most valid inference would be that:
    a. the teacher is using wait-time properly.
    b. students are not responding properly.
    c. questions are being asked of only a few students.
    d. questions are probably at the knowledge level.
25. There is some research to support the conclusion that:
    a. a low level question will get a high level response if you only wait long enough.
    b. a low level question with a very short wait-time elicits a high level student response.
    c. a longer wait-time has no effect on knowledge based questions, i.e., the students will still answer at the knowledge level.
    d. a longer wait-time has absolutely no effect on any kind of teacher question.

Answer Sheet for Chapter 6

1.	a	14.	d
2.	b	15.	a
3.	c	16.	b
4.	d	17.	a
5.	d	18.	b
6.	c	19.	c
7.	a	20.	d
8.	b	21.	c
9.	b	22.	a
10.	a	23.	b
11.	c	24.	d
12.	c	25.	c
13.	d		

Overhead Transparency Masters for Chapter 6

The following transparency masters are included at the end of the Manual to assist you in presenting concepts from Chapter 6.

 6-1. Research on Questioning
 6-2. Basic Questioning Categories
 6-3. Concept Mapping
 6-4. Appropriate Questioning Behavior
 6-5. Technical and Humane Considerations
 6-6. Wait-Time 1
 6-7. Wait-Time 2
 6-8. Wait-Time Rationale
 6-9. Wait-Time--Teacher Payoffs
6-10. Wait-Time--Student Payoffs
6-11. Prompting
6-12. Review Questions
6-13. Teacher Idiosyncrasies

CHAPTER 7

DECISIONS ABOUT DISCUSSIONS

Overview

Chapter 7 provides a thorough introduction to the classroom uses of eight types of small-group discussions and cooperative learning. Successful acquisition of the instructional strategies associated with group learning gives teachers a powerful teaching tool. Conversely, poor discussion techniques produce classroom disasters. Because techniques are so important, the chapter is designed to provide your students with (1) a conceptual base, (2) definitive teaching guidelines, and (3) first-hand experiences.

It is important for your students to master the conceptual basis of group learning; especially for cooperative learning. Cooperative learning may be so different from your students' experiences that a visit to a classroom using cooperative learning is suggested. Or, bring in some teachers who can describe how it works in their classes.

We actually teach each small-group discussion type with the method described in this chapter. Topics can be selected from the chapter or from local or state issues. Do model the guidelines suggested for specific discussion types. We also have our students analyze each discussion. Possibly the most meaningful part of the activity is the evaluation phase. Teachers are not accustomed to evaluating group processes, thus first-hand experience with process evaluation is crucial for experiential learning.

Student Activities

1. The students need to experience a Phillips 66 discussion group, and should be able to critique that type of group. To conduct the activity, divide the class into groups of 6, or as close to 6 as possible. The more diverse each group the better. Follow the technique described in the text. Orally state the problem/situation to be discussed. For example: "From your own experiences in school, what were the two worst consequences about the ways teachers use group discussions?" "What were the two best consequences?" Each recorder then shares the findings with the class.

2. The students need to understand how to organize a class for cooperative learning. Provide the class with real or hypothetical set of

student scores or achievement data. The scores should span a fairly wide
range. If possible, provide learner objectives for the topics being covered.
        Divide the class into groups of 6 to 8 and select a leader. State
that they will be doing a simulation. They are to plan 3 cooperative learning
activities using the data provided. For each learning activity they must:
(a) explain how they formed the learning groups, (b) explain the process or
product objective, and (c) provide a brief description of the activity. Each
group then shares their results with other groups.
        Each group needs to evaluate their process. Figure 7-4 would be an
appropriate form to use.

Annotated References for Student Study

        1. Lewandowski, Jean A. (1989, Spring). "Using Peer Forums to
Motivate Students." Teaching Exceptional Children, 21(3), 14-15.
        The author provides an excellent example of using panel discussions
with high school youth who were in her "resource room." Following a model
similar to what is proposed in Chapter 7, she found that being in a panel
(Forum) students were motivated to work harder, be better prepared and had a
higher regard for quality of work.

        2. Smagovinsky, Peter. (1989, February). "Small Groups: A New
Dimension in Learning." English Journal, 78(2), 67-70.
        Teaching units on literature can be made more interactive by combining
whole class instruction and small group learning. Smagovinsky illustrates a
four-step process that can be applied: (1) introductory work, (2) study of
symbolics, (3) synthesis of ideas, and (4) student independence. This paper
strongly implies endorsement of our emphasis on small group learning and real
discussions in the classroom.

        3. Shermis, S. Samuel. (1988, Spring). "Teaching About Intervention
in the Social Studies Classroom." Social Science Record, 25(2), 67-72.
        Shermis takes the historical concept of national intervention and
shows how social studies teachers can provide provocative questions for
students that promote high levels of thinking and decision-making.
        This paper is excellent for task groups, panels, or inquiry groups.

        4. Wasserman, Selma. (1989, Summer). "Children Working in Groups?
It Doesn't Work!" Childhood Education, 65(4), 201-205.
        Don't let the title deceive you. This is an interesting case study of
how a teacher in suburban New York City school successfully implemented
cooperative learning with 36, yes, 36 sixth graders in one class! This paper
illustrates the initial frustrations and ultimate success the teacher had when
using one of the fastest growing teaching strategies.

Chapter 7 Test Questions

1. Process objectives rely on:
   a. learning behavioral outcomes.
   b. experiential activities.
   c. evaluation processes.
   d. values to be learned.
2. Which of the following is not a strength of small-group discussions?
   a. Encourages students to state personal opinions.
   b. Some students become group leaders.
   c. Facilitates memorization.
   d. Facilitates communication among students.
3. Evaluation of group processes is important because:
   a. feedback can help students be better participants.
   b. students are concerned about grades.
   c. all outcomes need to be measured.
   d. administrators are concerned about accountability.
4. The teacher's role in setting up a class to conduct discussions is best described as:
   a. noninvolved--the teacher simply stands back and watches.
   b. plans all the topics to be discussed.
   c. prepares the class with discussion skills.
   d. determines the tasks for every phase for all discussions.
5. A teaching technique which provides the best opportunity for developing learner spontaneity is:
   a. Phillips 66.
   b. tutorial.
   c. task groups.
   d. brainstorming.
6. Since listening is so important when using discussion groups, probably the best teacher technique is to:
   a. practice the directions first on fellow teachers.
   b. give directions slowly but refuse to repeat them.
   c. ask if there are any questions after giving directions.
   d. call on one or two students to paraphrase directions after giving them, then clear up misconceptions.
7. In group activity, the most important reason for the teacher to be an active observer is to:
   a. assess and guide individual and group growth in participatory skills.
   b. see that they are recording what is going on.
   c. select appropriate leaders.
   d. direct student plans for class presentations.

8. A process objective:
   a. requires the prescribing of exact learner behavior.
   b. requires the learner to participate in some technique, interaction, or strategy.
   c. is the basis for development of hierarchy.
   d. has no significance regarding the topic for discussion.

9. Which of the following statements is not used in defining the discussion process?
   a. Formal learning concepts.
   b. A small number of students (4-8) meeting together.
   c. Introduction, exchange, and evaluation of ideas.
   d. Verbal interaction, both objective and emotional.

10. The authors of your text point out that self-serving roles in a discussion group are neither positive or constructive to the groups. Which of the following is not a self-serving role?
    a. The interpreter.
    b. The dominator.
    c. The blocker.
    d. The recognition seeker.

11. Matthew B. Miles emphasizes five main functions of the small group leader that all students can practice at any time during the discussion. Which of the following is not one of these?
    a. Evaluation.
    b. Supporting.
    c. Manipulating.
    d. Regulating.

12. Panel discussions:
    a. require previous research or study.
    b. are those in which the teacher decides the topic.
    c. are spontaneously generated.
    d. require virtually no skills on the part of students.

13. The best seating arrangement for group discussions is:
    a. traditional rows.
    b. non-ordered random placement.
    c. semi-circular.
    d. student self-placement to enhance individuality.

14. One major goal of discussion group evaluation is:
    a. creativity.
    b. clarifying issues.
    c. to determine productivity.
    d. to provide summative evaluation.

15. When deciding to use cooperative learning in your classroom, the three types of evaluation or accountability focus on:
    a. the teacher, the topic, and the group.
    b. the individual, the group, and the process.
    c. the textbook, the test, and the readings.
    d. the seating, the climate, and the group.

16. The concept of group cohesion includes the three crucial elements of:
    a. role, leadership, and purpose.
    b. purpose, structure, and influence.
    c. influence, unity, and feedback.
    d. unity, purpose, and attraction.

17. Three important behaviors for a tutorial group leader to use are:
    a. questioning, criticizing, and praising.
    b. questioning, providing feedback, and encouraging.
    c. questioning, lecturing, and evaluating.
    d. questioning, evaluation, and criticizing.

18. Which type of small-group discussion would be most likely to use a physical model?
    a. brainstorming.
    b. simulation.
    c. panel.
    d. role-playing.

19. Which type of small-group discussion is most likely to require the skillful asking of questions?
    a. Task.
    b. Simulation.
    c. Brainstorming.
    d. Inquiry.

20. Cooperative learning groups are structured to have:
    a. students with varying achievement levels.
    b. low achieving students.
    c. high achieving students.
    d. students who can learn without the teacher's help.

21. The best reason for considering cooperative learning is that it:
    a. increases the ability to brainstorm.
    b. decreases the need to memorize.
    c. decreases the need to learn questioning skills.
    d. increases cognitive achievement.

22. To use small-groups successfully, the teacher's role can be best described as:
    a. leader and evaluator.
    b. observer and recorder.
    c. facilitator.
    d. resource person.

Answer Sheet for Chapter 7

1.	b	12.	a
2.	c	13.	c
3.	a	14.	c
4.	c	15.	b
5.	d	16.	d
6.	d	17.	b
7.	a	18.	b
8.	b	19.	d
9.	a	20.	a
10.	a	21.	d
11.	c	22.	c

Overhead Transparency Masters for Chapter 7

The following transparency masters are included at the end of the Manual to assist you in presenting concepts from Chapter 7.

7-1. Small Groups
7-2. Small Group Discussions
7-3. Classroom Atmosphere
7-4. Critical Concepts
7-5. Small Group Types
7-6. Cooperative Learning
7-7. Cooperative Learning Processes
7-8. Encouraging Small Groups

CHAPTER 8

DECIDING TO USE INQUIRY

Overview

Chapter 8 provides a detailed rationale supporting the use of John Dewey's classic ideal of problem-solving. We illustrate many ways of incorporating inquiry-oriented lessons in any classroom. This statement leads to Chapter 9 which expands the notion of teaching for thinking and understanding student learning styles.

It is imperative to discuss and to expand the need for systematic development of student inquiry skills. One assignment won't do it in the K-12 sector. When presenting this chapter, we suggest using the various inquiry techniques so that class members can participate in an inquiry mode.

Student Activities

1. The use of data is an important skill when teaching inquiry skills. By using local newspapers an unguided inductive inquiry session can be demonstrated.

Divide the class into groups of four students. Each group should select a recorder and a leader. Provide each group with eight to ten daily issues of a local newspaper. Have each group make generalizations about (1) editorial policy, (2) advertisements, and (3) classified ads based on the information they find in those papers.

Generalizations should then be reported to the entire class. Each group must support its generalizations with evidence or data about the specific issues. Discuss how the unguided inquiry model may be useful in their respective fields of study.

2. Divide the class into small groups of four to six. Each group is given the challenge to define a problem that affects them personally at the college or university. Once each group has a problem operationally defined, ask them to devise a plan that uses inquiry concepts to solve or reconcile the identified problem.

Annotated References for Student Study

1. Galbraith-Jones, Marian. (1987, October). "The Famous Authors Convention." English Journal, 76(6), 64-66.
A very creative, role-playing technique is described by Galbraith-Jones. Middle school students study one author in-depth and then become that author for one day at the simulated "Famous Authors Convention."

2. Kleg, Milton. (1988, Fall). "Rights in Conflict: An Inquiry Simulation on Smoking." Social Science Record, 25(2), 30-33.
John Dewey's idea of a problem is the theoretical undergirding of this piece which combines a simulation device on smoking with the scientific method of problem-solving. Using the issue of smoking should provide very interesting discussions.

3. Smith, Michael W. and George Hillocks, Jr. (1989, February). "What Inquiry Writers Need to Know." English Journal 78(2), 58-63.
Citing an example from one middle school and ten high school classes, the authors illustrate how the basic elements of inquiry (as espoused in Chapter 8) can be used most effectively to improve student writing. "Few findings in educational research are unequivocal," wrote Smith and Hillocks and then concluded that, "One of them appears to be the power of inquiry-based activities in improving composition."

4. Wilen, William W. and Patrick McKenrick. (1989, January-February). "Individualized Inquiry: Encouraging Able Students to Investigate." Social Studies, 80(1), 36-39.
While we suggest inquiry teaching and learning for all students, the authors provide a case study showing how to challenge the most capable students by using an inquiry approach with social studies instruction.

Chapter 8 Test Questions

1. To convert "knowledge" to an inquiry learning experience, a teacher must:
   a. use one of Suchman's techniques.
   b. prepare the student with prerequisite learning experiences.
   c. conduct one discussion on inquiry so students will respond with the correct answers.
   d. anticipate all possible responses so that adequate preparation can be made beforehand.

2. Inquiry process requires interaction between:
   a. teacher and students.
   b. teaching materials, teacher and students.
   c. students and materials.
   d. none of the above.

3. As a social studies teacher, you read a recent headline in the paper that stated, "Blunders Tied to MX Missile Vote." To use this headline as an inquiry device, you might begin with:
   a. explaining what was meant by the MX.
   b. describing the blunders that were involved in the MX vote.
   c. asking the class what they think are some of the circumstances that have led to this headline.
   d. asking only those students who had read the article to respond.

4. In any inquiry model, all questions concerning events or data are:
   a. asked by the teacher and answered by the students.
   b. answered with a yes or no by the teacher.
   c. asked by the student, responded to by the teacher, and then the teacher asks a question of the student.
   d. none of the above.

5. When using unguided inductive inquiry:
   a. the generalizations are discovered by the student, and may be rather unlimited.
   b. the objective is to arrive at one generalization.
   c. there is usually a limited number of generalizations.
   d. materials are not essential to the success of the experience.

6. In an inductive model of inquiry, there is usually:
   a. no concept being learned at all.
   b. one correct answer.
   c. a generalization given to the students so that they may test its validity.
   d. no answer listed.

7. A student of yours sends in an idea to the Microsoft Corporation (a computer software company). The idea is a new process for graphing statistical analyses. This discovery would be classified as:
    a. an absolute discovery.
    b. an application of guided inductive discovery.
    c. a relative discovery.
    d. a simulated discovery.

8. Which statement below is **NOT** a characteristic of inductive inquiry teaching?
    a. Teachers encourage a number of responses from students.
    b. Students must be taught process associated with inquiry.
    c. Solutions to the problems should be found in student textbooks.
    d. Students at all levels of learning can benefit from inquiry.

9. As a teacher, you provide a set of materials for the students to analyze. You expect the students to identify not more than five generalizations. You are likely using:
    a. unguided deductive reasoning.
    b. unguided inductive.
    c. guided inductive.
    d. guided deductive.

10. Which truncated set of steps is the most appropriate for problem-solving or inquiry?
    a. Make generalizations, collect data, change conclusions.
    b. Collect data, make hypotheses, define terms.
    c. Define problem, collect data, evaluate data.
    d. Establish limits, fit data to hypotheses, make conclusions.

11. Which questioning techniques would be most appropriate for most inquiry lessons?
    a. Ask divergent, convergent and evaluative questions.
    b. Use questions requiring memory only.
    c. Involve each student in questioning as little as possible.
    d. Seek out those who are intrinsically motivated and ask them questions.

12. There is some evidence to show that inquiry:
    a. is always inferior to other types of learning techniques.
    b. is often superior to other types of techniques of instruction.
    c. is neither inferior or superior to other types.
    d. cannot be used effectively by beginning teachers.

13. Critics of schools state that one of the following is overemphasized to the detriment of the others.
    a. Opportunity for free thought and expression.
    b. Teaching through discovery, which wastes time.
    c. Discussion techniques, small group problem-solving and panel presentations.
    d. The lower cognitive objectives of Bloom's Taxonomy.

14. Citing his criteria for problem-solving, you agree that John Dewey had a sound theory regarding the subject. Which criterion would support your decision from the list below?
    a. Problems are only relevant to the student.
    b. Problems are only relevant to the teacher and the broader culture.
    c. Problems should be significant to the culture as well as the learner.
    d. The type of problems being solved are unimportant; it is the process that is important.

15. If you as a teacher have decided to use inquiry strategies in your teaching, you will assume that:
    a. inquiry requires a greater amount of time to achieve instructional objectives than direct instruction.
    b. inquiry will require less time to achieve instructional objectives than direct instruction strategies.
    c. inquiry requires about the same amount of time to achieve learning objectives.
    d. inquiry cannot have instructional objectives as it is open-ended.

16. Inquiry, simulations, and educational games are useful for motivating students because:
    a. they are idealistic, and do not pertain to real life or relevant events.
    b. they are active participants in learning.
    c. they provide extrinsic motivation.
    d. they are easier.

17. Which of the following is **NOT** a component of a guided inductive lesson?
    a. Students moving in unison through the lesson.
    b. A few specific solutions to the problem.
    c. Students using independent research.
    d. The teacher seldom intervening in the process once it gets going.

18. You decide to involve your students in a community project that is aimed at providing a cleaner environment around the school. Which technique would be the most effective one?
    a. Absolute discovery.
    b. Problem-solving.
    c. Simulation.
    d. Unguided inductive.

19. A discrepant event is discussed by your class. What technique is the best one to employ so that student learning is maximized?
    a. Hypothesis testing.
    b. Unguided inductive.
    c. Guided problem-solving.
    d. Relative discovery.

20. Which technique directs students toward a particular set of generalizations by the use of learning activities which stress the use of observation, inference, hypothesis building, and generalizations?
    a. Deductive.
    b. Guided deductive.
    c. Unguided inductive.
    d. No answer listed.

21. All conclusions gained through inquiry are usually considered to be final.
    a. True
    b. False

22. When a teacher incorporates inquiry learning, then the number of interactions tends to decline.
    a. True
    b. False

23. The best way to incorporate any inquiry lesson into your teaching is to provide learners with the solutions and then let the learners discuss them.
    a. True
    b. False

24. Magazines are a very poor medium to be used when incorporating inquiry techniques in a classroom.
    a. True
    b. False

25. If one summarizes all aspects of the process we call inquiry, then one must conclude that inquiry is the best technique by which to learn factual information.
    a. True
    b. False

Answer Sheet for Chapter 8

1.	b		14.	c
2.	d		15.	a
3.	c		16.	b
4.	d		17.	a
5.	a		18.	b
6.	d		19.	a
7.	a		20.	c
8.	c		21.	b
9.	c		22.	b
10.	c		23.	b
11.	a		24.	b
12.	b		25.	b
13.	d			

Overhead Transparency Masters for Chapter 8

The following transparency masters are included at the end of the Manual to assist you in presenting concepts from Chapter 8.

8-1. Inquiry Models
8-2. Guided Inductive Inquiry
8-3. Unguided Inductive Inquiry
8-4. Problem-Solving
8-5. Problem-Solving
8-6. John Dewey's Concept of a Problem
8-7. Discovery Learning
8-8. Assumptions About Inquiry

CHAPTER 9

DECISIONS TO ENCOURAGE CRITICAL THINKING

Overview

Although concerned with two major topics--thinking processes and
learning styles--Chapter 9 emphasizes one major issue: How can teachers best
help students to improve their ability to understand. Understanding, of
course, is basic to functioning effectively both in and out of school.
"Thinking" seems almost synonomous with understanding, while a knowledge of
the similarities and differences in how students learn can be critical in
determining if they learn. The two topics of thinking and learning styles are
two components of the same issue--understanding.

These topics lend themselves to small group discussions and many
suggestions for such are offered within the chapter. One instructional
approach seems especially pertinent. Use variations of the oral problem
solving activity to have students explain their understandings of major
chapter topics, thus engaging in a high-level thinking activity as well as
reinforcing their own learning.

Student Activities

1. The following activity is intended to help students identify and
practice specific thinking skills such as observing, categorizing, inferring,
seeking assumptions, and generalizing. Undoubtedly, other thought processes
are involved and instructors are urged to help students recognize whichever
ones seem relevant.

The first exercise is based upon a painting which students examine for
several days as they answer questions about it. Many paintings could be
useful, but realistic portrayals of an easily-recognizable scene or event seem
the most effective. The painting which one of the writers has used frequently
is "Downing the Nigh Leader" by Frederick Remington--a vivid portrayal of
Indians attacking a stage coach.

The exercise has been done in the following way:
a. The painting is displayed for several days in a place where
    students can view it whenever they wish--a hallway, perhaps,
    or an office door.

b. Students are given the question sheet (below) to guide their study of the painting.

c. Students are encouraged to work together on the questions, particularly to discuss possible answers and the reasoning that leads them.

d. On the day the assignment is handed in, hold a class discussion of the possible answers, the evidence to support, and the reasoning that developed them.

Painting Exercise. Use the painting on my office door for your answers. For those questions which ask, "How do you know?", state which details in the painting support your answer.

1. Who is the artist?
2. What is the painting titled?
3. What is the general subject of the painting?
4. What is the geographical setting? How do you know?
5. What time period is depicted? How do you know?
6. What groups of people are represented? Evidence?
7. What, specifically, is happening? How do you know?
8. What does the title mean? How do you know?
9. Which group is the aggressor in the painting? Evidence?
10. What will be the probable outcome of this activity? Why? Evidence?
11. Which questions fit into the following categories? (A question may fall into more than 1 category.)
    (a) Convergent
    (b) Divergent
    (c) Knowledge
    (d) Analysis
    (e) Evaluation
12. In a brief paragraph (1/2 page), explain how this lesson reinforces particular thinking processes (specify the skills or processes).

2. The second activity which is a variation of Whimbey's "Oral Problem Solving" clarifies and reinforces any complex assignment or segment of learning. The example to be used would be prepared or duplicated by the instructor and distributed in a student handout.

Oral problem solving. Organizing, summarizing, and synthesizing your ideas is an effective learning tool. It is also one of the most effective methods for promoting and improving critical thought processes.

Students should be given frequent opportunity to "think about what they say" and then "say what they think," whether in speech or writing.

The following exercise is one way of using these suggestions to help students clarify and focus their thinking in relation to assignments.

Purposes of activity. The purpose of this activity is to:
1. Clarify the "rationale Paper" assignment.
2. Practice an "Oral Problem Solving" method.
Process. There are five processes to do this activity:
1. Group into "two's,"
2. One person is the "solver," the other is the listener/critic,"
3. "Solver" explains the following three aspects.
    (a) I understand the Rationale Paper assignment to be as
         follows:
    (b) I am approaching or doing the assignment in these ways:
    (c) I am unclear or have problems in these areas:
4. "Listener/critic"
    (a) Summarizes points a, b, c above for "Solver."
    (b) Asks for clarification as needed.
5. Reverse roles
    Time. Fifteen (15) minutes for each person.

Annotated References for Student Study

    1. Clarkin, Maura. (1988, March). "Frank Stella." Art Education,
41(2), 25-26.
    This is a one-page lesson plan to guide a critical study of Stella's
abstract painting "Hockenheim." It is an excellent model of a lesson plan
devoted to critical thought, as well as a much-needed example of integrating
aesthetics into the curriculum. Such lesson plans, devoted to particular
artistic works, are a regular feature of Art Education under the heading
"Instructional Resources: Technology."

    2. Ennis, Robert H. (1989, April). "Critical Thinking and Subject
Specificity: Clarification and Needed Research." Educational Researcher,
18(3), 4-10.
    Ennis provides critical examination of two major issues in thought
instruction. First, should thinking be taught as a separate course, be
infused "into existing courses, or be taught as a combination of the above
methods. Second, Ennis examines the term "subject specificity," noting its
relationship to instructional method, difficulties of definition, and areas
for further research. This is an excellent article to extend theoretical
understandings of the chapter.

    3. Eulie, Joseph. (1988, November/December). "Teaching Under-
standing and Developing Critical Thinking." The Social Studies, 79(6),
260-265.
    Eulie offers an infusion of critical thinking instruction into any
subject (social studies is illustrated) through the "developmental lesson."

An excellent link between theory and practice is offered with four sample lesson plans.

4.   Wassermann, Selma. (1989, January). "Reflections on Measuring Thinking, While Listening to Mozart's 'Jupiter' Symphony." Phi Delta Kappan, 70(5), 365-370.

Wasserman thoughtfully explores the ambiguities of the concept "thinking," and then develops in-depth the harm that may follow from attempts to measure thought in terms of numerical scores. The article is an excellent extension of the chapter's discussion of evaluation.

Chapter 9 Test Questions

1. Which general skill can be taught to improve effective thinking?
    a. Comparing and contrasting.
    b. Distinguishing relevant from irrelevant data.
    c. Identifying assumptions.
    d. All of the above.
2. One significant reason why schools should teach thinking is to help students become better in:
    a. test taking.
    b. fact finding.
    c. personal development.
    d. no answer listed.
3. There are at least three types of thinking commonly distinguished:
    a. critical, problem solving, and creative.
    b. subliminal, subconscious, and creative.
    c. conscious, intuitive, and critical.
    d. metacognitive, realistic, and creative.
4. Critical thinking is distinguished by being:
    a. non-evaluative.
    b. essentially evaluative.
    c. at a low cognitive level.
    d. intuitive.
5. In planning a lesson for problem solving, the lesson design should involve:
    a. systematic analysis.
    b. reflective skepticism.
    c. identification of assumptions.
    d. all of the above.
6. A student that demonstrates divergent thinking may be said to be utilizing:
    a. subliminal thought.
    b. deductive analysis.
    c. creative thinking.
    d. inductive analysis.
7. A classroom discussion centered around problem solving might best utilize:
    a. creative thinking and critical problem solving skills.
    b. factual information and brainstorming.
    c. strict focus upon the textbook.
    d. teacher-dominated questioning.

8. Which questioning technique would be most appropriate for most problem-solving lessons?
   a. Use questions requiring only memory responses.
   b. Ask divergent questions and convergent questions.
   c. Involve each student in the questioning as little as possible.
   d. Seek only those students who are interested in the problem and ask them questions.

9. A teacher that plans a lesson on "thinking" should anticipate receiving what from students?
   a. The correct answer in one or two cases.
   b. Virtually no student responses.
   c. Classroom discipline problems due to the integrations.
   d. "Possible" answers instead of "the" answer.

10. A true false test is most likely to be designed to:
    a. critical thinking.
    b. creative thinking.
    c. factual thinking.
    d. problem solving.

11. Dunn and Dunn identified four key dimensions on which learning styles differ. Which of the following is not one of the dimensions?
    a. The environment.
    b. Emotional support.
    c. The financial success of the district.
    d. Sociological composition.

12. The perceptual tendencies for learning styles described by Woolfolk identify two distinct groups of people. The two groups can be classified as:
    a. knowledge/evaluation types.
    b. field dependent/field independent types.
    c. type X and type Y.
    d. social and non-social types.

13. Gregorc's approach to learning styles can be subdivided into perceptual preferences of:
    a. concrete/abstract.
    b. cognitive/abstract.
    c. visual/motor.
    d. logical/emotional.

14. Which is the best example of critical thinking:
    a. answering true-false questions on a test.
    b. calculating an answer from a given formula.
    c. determining the best of three possible solutions to a problem.
    d. performing a science-text experiment and recording the results.

15. An example of metacognition is:
    a. considering the thinking processes in solving a calculus problem.
    b. brainstorming in a small group.
    c. making choices on a complex multiple choice test.
    d. learning vocabulary in a foreign language.
16. Thinking processes are:
    a. rarely found in "slow" students.
    b. innate to humans.
    c. readily observed in "gifted" students.
    d. genetically determined and incapable of change.
17. Which attitude is opposed to critical thought:
    a. reflective scepticism.
    b. suspended judgment.
    c. rejection of opposing data.
    d. acceptance of ambiguity.
18. Thinking processes are best measured by:
    a. essay tests.
    b. anecdotal records.
    c. oral examination.
    d. variety of written and non-written indicators.
19. An "infused" instructional approach to thinking processes suggests:
    a. devoting a special time in several classes for thinking instruction.
    b. creating a separate class for thinking instruction.
    c. including thinking instruction in all classes.
    d. using parents, administrators, and aids to provide thinking instruction.
20. Which item is least characteristic of a "thoughtful" classroom environment:
    a. non-judgmental acceptance of all contributions.
    b. an emphases upon correct responses.
    c. encouragement of divergent thinking.
    d. much interaction among students.
21. Information processing psychology suggests that "learning" is best characterized by:
    a. associating appropriate stimuli and responses.
    b. rejecting obviously inappropriate stimuli.
    c. the results of continuous repetition.
    d. adapting new experience to existing schema.
22. Oral problem solving is appropriate:
    a. only to story problems in math.
    b. to both story problems and abstract formuli in math.
    c. to science classes as well as math classes.
    d. to some learning in every class.

23. Thinking instruction should be emphasized:
    a. each day.
    b. only on alternate days to avoid repetition.
    c. weekly, to enhance long-term retention.
    d. randomly, to support an intermittent reinforcement.
24. Concept understanding is best measured by:
    a. true-false items.
    b. student-generated examples.
    c. distinguishing correct from incorrect definitions.
    d. random questioning of several students.
25. The most important factor in thinking instruction is:
    a. a teacher who understands and practices thoughtful behavior.
    b. students who are highly motivated.
    c. students from a rich experiential background.
    d. strong administrative support.

Answer Sheet for Chapter 9

1.	d	14.	c
2.	c	15.	a
3.	a	16.	b
4.	b	17.	c
5.	d	18.	d
6.	c	19.	c
7.	a	20.	b
8.	b	21.	d
9.	d	22.	d
10.	c	23.	a
11.	c	24.	b
12.	b	25.	a
13.	a		

Overhead Transparency Masters for Chapter 9

The following transparency masters are included at the end of the Manual to assist you in presenting concepts from Chapter 9.

9-1. Critical Thought
9-2. Critical Thinking Attitude
9-3. Creative Thought
9-4. Assumptions for Critical Thinking
9-5. Enhancing Classroom Thinking
9-6. Encouraging Thinking Behaviors
9-7. Encouraging Thinking Behaviors
9-8. Three Teaching Concepts
9-9. Four Learning Styles

CHAPTER 10

DECIDING HOW TO MANAGE A CLASS

Overview

Chapter Ten provides an introduction to the alternatives for classroom management. We hope prospective teachers leave this chapter with some idea of the many variables that confront them in the classroom. We also desire to generate the beginning of a philosophy for approaching management issues. It is important for the new teacher to understand that research can suggest classroom-tested applications which result in student learning through a humanely managed classroom environment.

New teachers should also learn that uniformed discovery of classroom management practices is a costly luxury. Students lose valuable learning time, the teacher loses credibility, and the support of the paying public is greatly diminished. In this chapter, we hope to "jump start" new teachers toward selected successful generic management practices. Each new technique can eventually be developed into a mature approach in classroom management.

Student Activities

1. Each student should establish 4 to 5 rules of basic classroom management and a strategy for explaining the rules to a chosen group of students. Sub-divide the class into groups and have each student simulate their opening classroom management address to a new class.

2. Each student should explain the processes that will be used during the first month of school to reinforce the rules established during the first week.

Annotated References for Student Study

1. Educational Leadership, (1989, March), 46(6), 2-85.
The entire March issue is devoted to topics that are directly related to classroom management. Papers address gender issues, gifted and slow learners and equity, disruptive students, and learning styles. This number could easily be utilized as the basic resource for Chapter 10.

2.   Helmke, Andreas and F. W. Schrader. (1988, November/December).
"Successful Student Practice During Seatwork: Efficient Management and Active
Supervision Not Enough." Journal of Educational Research, 82(2), 70-75.
         How does a teacher manage a classroom during seatwork periods to
ensure success? Andreas and Schrader have determined that frequency of
practice in itself was not related to achievement, but other factors were
influential. The authors suggest practice, management, and active supervision
that supports and corrects students in a discreet manner determined achievement.

3.   Livingston, Carol and Hilda Borko. (1989, July-August). "Expert-
Novice Differences in Teaching: A Cognitive Analysis and Implications for
Teacher Education." Journal of Teacher Education, 40(4), 36-42.
         The authors provide a thought-provoking discussion of the differences
of expert and novice teachers and the implications for instruction and management. They conclude that "novices may possess insufficient knowledge and
skills to adopt the routines and actions of expert teachers or to learn
effectively from their own experiences in the classroom."

4.   Murphy, Joseph and Karen Decker. (1989, May/June). "Teachers'
Use of Homework in High Schools." Journal of Educational Research, 82(5),
261-269.
         The authors investigate how teachers assign, review, and grade student
work. The purposes of homework are explained and student responses to homework were evaluated through the eyes of their teachers. This paper is an
excellent stimulus for small group discussions.

Chapter 10 Test Questions

1. The Gallup polls have consistently demonstrated that the people of this country:
    a. do not believe the schools have any discipline problems.
    b. recognize the discipline problems, but consider them to be minor.
    c. perceive discipline to be a key problem in schools.
    d. believe discipline problems can be easily reconciled.
2. Generally, the most effective management strategy will be the one that:
    a. provides an opportunity for lengthy dialogue between student and teacher.
    b. produces the desired results with the lowest expenditure of the teacher's time and effort.
    c. involves the principal in the discipline act.
    d. provides punishment for the student.
3. Regarding discipline or classroom management, the text supports all but one position.
    a. There is one good, acceptable method of maintaining classroom discipline, teachers should use it.
    b. Some teachers tend to contribute to the problem.
    c. There are several techniques that can be appropriately applied.
    d. Several techniques are based on theory: you can find out what works for you in practice.
4. Behavior modification will be effective if the following guideline is followed:
    a. work on one behavior at a time.
    b. use the same reinforcer for each class member.
    c. never use group pressure.
    d. never use negative reinforcement.
5. Democratic discipline suggests that:
    a. no rules are permissible, for they imply authority and authority has no place in a democratic classroom.
    b. rule making should be limited to items that hinge on state laws.
    c. rule making should reflect rational explanations of behaviors.
    d. because the teacher realizes that the students are mere juveniles, he or she makes the rule, which the student must endorse.
6. Reality therapy is based on all but one of the following assumptions or principles:
    a. punishment is an effective reinforcing technique.
    b. excuses are not accepted for not reaching goals.
    c. children from disadvantaged homes are responsible for their behavior.
    d. remaining distant and objective is in opposition to applying the principles.

7. When conflict is defined, ideas brainstormed, solutions listed and discussed, solutions picked, strategies developed and implemented, and finally evaluated, the method used is:
    a. Gordon's no lose strategy.
    b. Rudolf Drickurs' approach.
    c. Maslow's Hierarchy of Needs.
    d. Good's communication model.
8. Teachers often unintentionally express their feeling of:
    a. low expectations for student success.
    b. negative feelings towards students.
    c. lack of awareness of student needs.
    d. all of the above.
9. Classroom rules clearly posted and enforced is an example of:
    a. desist strategy.
    b. common sense.
    c. assertive discipline.
    d. effective schools practices.
10. Teacher interference in stopping undesired behavior should always be:
    a. at the least point of resistance.
    b. a lowest level of force.
    c. verbal.
    d. threatening.

    Below is a series of "mini" cases. In each case, the teacher, Pat Taylor, takes some action. You must determine what management strategy was employed. On your answer sheet mark each case with an A for behavior modification; a B for desist strategy; a C for reality therapy; and a D for no systematic method being followed.

11. Both Charlie and Charlene (students) have written out a detailed plan of how they will behave in very productive ways. And, just as you would expect, neither follows the plan. Pat calls them in for a conference. Everyone is "loose" and there are "no fingers pointed." Charlie and Charlene write out a new plan for instructional improvement. Pat even reads the plan to the class. What system is being used in this case?
    A--Behavior Mod
    B--Desist Therapy
    C--Reality Therapy
    D--No System

12. Pat was transferred to the junior high to help out with a "tough" class. A meeting was held between Pat and the two counselors and the vice-principal. This group planned a technique that would be applied for effective management. All agreed that Pat would have to use a variety of verbal and nonverbal techniques to be successful with the class. This action is what technique?
    A--Behavior Mod
    B--Desist Therapy
    C--Reality Therapy
    D--No System

13. Pat has had much trouble with Randy E. No homework has been handed in for six to seven assignments. Pat discusses Randy's problem with him. Randy writes out a plan to finish his assignments. What strategy is being employed?
    A--Behavior Mod
    B--Desist Therapy
    C--Reality Therapy
    D--No System

14. Susan J. is a consistent note-writer. These notes "break-up" the class almost daily. Pat tends to read them aloud to the class when inter-cepted. One day a colleague told Pat to ignore the whole behavior of Susan, and to comment favorably when Susan is attending to business. What technique is being employed after the discussion with the colleague.
    A--Behavior Mod
    B--Desist Therapy
    C--Reality Therapy
    D--No System

15. BoBo Smith, 216 pound football player, was whispering a sweet nothing to his classmate across the row. Both sit in the last row. Pat notices this and gives both BoBo and friend a chilling glance--"double whammy" if you will. What strategy is being used?
    A--Behavior Mod
    B--Desist Therapy
    C--Reality Therapy
    D--No System

16. The class has been "acting up" for about a week. Pat finally states that if the entire class starts to (1) hand in work (100% of them); (2) stops "goofing off" during the study and attend to their lessons (100% of them) for the next four days, then Pat will allow a ten-minute "free period" on Friday. What strategy is being used?
    A--Behavior Mod
    B--Desist Therapy
    C--Reality Therapy
    D--No System

17. Mr. I. M. Grouchy, high school principal, enrolled for a summer session and, being a secondary teacher, just sat in on the Introduction to Teaching Strategies class. One classroom management system that was taken back to the high school entailed a new theory. I. M. told Pat that "more responsibility is needed" for high schoolers. Pat begins to discuss the concept of "responsibility" with the class. P. M. Farrah (a junior) suggests a set of responsibilities to be followed. Rosie C. (a senior) adds the idea of trying to work more productively. Ronnie B. (a junior) says "none of this stuff can work because nobody will follow responsibilities anyway." The discussion continues. A set of responsibilities are adopted. What strategy is being used?
    A--Behavior Mod
    B--Desist Therapy
    C--Reality Therapy
    D--No System

18. Pat returns from a seminar and reported to the principal and fellow colleagues that as a faculty, they must become aware of private and public communication dimensions of classroom management. What strategy are these concepts from?
    A--Behavior Mod
    B--Desist Therapy
    C--Reality Therapy
    D--No System

19. What advantage is there for imposed discipline over self-discipline systems?
    a. There are no advantages.
    b. Students know what is expected.
    c. The teacher has far more control over the class.
    d. The principal would suspend students who break your rules.

20. Classroom management would include all but one of the responses below.
    a. Teacher paces activities of class.
    b. Teacher plans for transitions.
    c. Teacher lowers student grade for misbehaving.
    d. Teacher continuously scans class for possible "problems."

Answer Sheet for Chapter 10

1.	c	11.	c
2.	b	12.	b
3.	a	13.	c
4.	a	14.	a
5.	c	15.	b
6.	a	16.	a
7.	a	17.	d
8.	d	18.	b
9.	d	19.	c
10.	b	20.	c

Overhead Transparency Masters for Chapter 10

The following transparency masters are included at the end of the Manual to assist you in presenting concepts from Chapter 10.

10-1. Reality Therapy Principles
10-2. Desist Strategies Dimensions
10-3. Desist Strategies
10-4. Behavior Modification
10-5. Assertive Discipline
10-6. Effective Classroom Management
10-7. Classroom Management

OVERHEAD TRANSPARENCY MASTERS

Chapter 1

1-1. Teacher as Decision-Maker
1-2. Understanding School Culture
1-3. Incentives and School Culture
1-4. Inviting Student Success
1-5. Effective Schools
1-6. Effective Schools
1-7. Emerging Instructional Issues

Chapter 2

2-1. Goals
2-2. Objectives
2-3. Performance Objectives
2-4. Rationale for Performance Objectives
2-5. Problems with Performance Objectives
2-6. Left Hemispheric Functions
2-7. Left Hemispheric Functions
2-8. Right Hemispheric Functions
2-9. Right Hemispheric Functions
2-10. Curriculum Alignment

Chapter 3

3-1. Models of Lesson Organization
3-2. Task Analysis
3-3. Concept Analysis
3-4. Advance Organizer
3-5. Diagnostic Prescriptive

Chapter 4

4-1. Cognitive Taxonomy
4-2. Knowledge
4-3. Comprehension
4-4. Application and Analysis
4-5. Synthesis
4-6. Evaluation
4-7. Affective Domain
4-8. Jewett and Mullan's Taxonomy

Chapter 5

5-1. Lesson-Planning Cycle
5-2. Lesson Implementation
5-3. Lesson Implementation
5-4. Instructional Procedures
5-5. Teacher Effectiveness
5-6. Rosenshine's Effective Teachers
5-7. ITIP Model
5-8. Direct Instruction
5-9. Direct Instruction--Weaknesses
5-10. Direct Instruction Steps

Chapter 6

6-1. Research on Questioning
6-2. Basic Questioning Categories
6-3. Concept Mapping
6-4. Appropriate Questioning Behavior
6-5. Technical and Humane Considerations
6-6. Wait-Time 1
6-7. Wait-Time 2
6-8. Wait-Time Rationale
6-9. Wait-Time--Teacher Payoffs
6-10. Wait-Time--Student Payoffs
6-11. Prompting
6-12. Review Questions
6-13. Teacher Idiosyncrasies

Chapter 7

7-1. Small Groups
7-2. Small Group Discussions
7-3. Classroom Atmosphere
7-4. Critical Concepts
7-5. Small Group Types
7-6. Cooperative Learning
7-7. Cooperative Learning Processes
7-8. Encouraging Small Groups

Chapter 8

8-1. Inquiry Models
8-2. Guided Inductive Inquiry
8-3. Unguided Inductive Inquiry
8-4. Problem-Solving
8-5. Problem-Solving
8-6. John Dewey's Concept of a Problem
8-7. Discovery Learning
8-8. Assumptions About Inquiry

Chapter 9

9-1. Critical Thought
9-2. Critical Thinking Attitude
9-3. Creative Thought
9-4. Assumptions for Critical Thinking
9-5. Enhancing Classroom Thinking
9-6. Encouraging Thinking Behaviors
9-7. Encouraging Thinking Behaviors
9-8. Three Teaching Concepts
9-9. Four Learning Styles

Chapter 10

10-1. Reality Therapy Principles
10-2. Desist Strategies Dimensions
10-3. Desist Strategies
10-4. Behavior Modification
10-5. Assertive Discipline
10-6. Effective Classroom Management
10-7. Classroom Management

Teacher As Decision Maker

- GOALS

- PERFORMANCE OBJECTIVES

- LEVELS OF INSTRUCTION

- PLANNING LESSONS

- TEACHING STRATEGIES

- CLASSROOM MANAGEMENT

- EVALUATION

Understanding School Culture

- SYSTEMS (ECOLOGY)

- UNCERTAINTY OF VALUES

- SCHOOL ETHOS

- SCHOOL VALUES

Incentives And School Culture

- INTRINSIC MOTIVATORS

- RECOGNITION

- APPRECIATION

- WORKING WITH PROFESSIONALS

Inviting Student Success

- INTENTIONALLY DISINVITING

- UNINTENTIONALLY DISINVITING

- UNINTENTIONALLY INVITING

- INTENTIONALLY INVITING

Orlich et al., <u>Teaching Strategies,</u> 3rd Ed., © 1990.

Effective Schools

- EXPECTATIONS

- CLASS ROUTINES AND PROCEDURES

- STANDARDS

- PEER INTERACTION

- STAGE SETTING

Effective Schools

- FOCUS ON INSTRUCTION

- LEARNING TIME

- RETEACHING

- TEACHER - STUDENT INTERACTIONS

- STUDENT REWARDS AND INCENTIVES

1-6 Orlich et al., Teaching Strategies, 3rd Ed., © 1990.

Emerging Instructional Issues

- TECHNOLOGY

- MATERIALS SELECTION

- BASICS

- PSYCHOLOGY FOR LEARNING

- TEACHER PREPARATION

- SCHOOL RESTRUCTURING

Goals

- IDEALS

- LONG - TERM

- DETERMINED SOCIALLY

- VALUE - LADEN

- NOT EASILY MEASURED OR EVALUATED

Objectives

- ACHIEVABLE EVENTS OR PRODUCTS

- SHORT - TERM

- SPECIFIC

- EASILY MEASURED OR EVALUATED

Performance Objectives

- CONDITION

- OBSERVABLE BEHAVIOR

- CRITERION MEASURE

Rationale for Performance Objectives

- ACCOUNTABILITY

- CURRICULUM ALIGNMENT

- HEMISPHERICITY

- COMPUTER AIDED INSTRUCTION

- MASTERY LEARNING

Problems with Performance Objectives

- CONFUSING INSTRUCTION AND CONDITION

- INCOMPLETE CRITERION STATEMENT

- INAPPROPRIATE CRITERION

- IRRELEVANT OBJECTIVES

Left Hemispheric Functions

- PROPOSITIONAL

- CATEGORICAL

- VERBAL

- ANALYTIC

- LOGICAL

Left Hemispheric Functions

- DETAIL ORIENTED

  - SYMBOLIC

  - CONVERGENT

  - ABSTRACT

  - INDUCTIVE

Right Hemispheric Functions

- INTUITIVE

- APPOSITIONAL

- PERCEPTUAL

- NON-VERBAL

- PATTERN ORIENTED

- SPATIAL

2-8 Orlich et al., <u>Teaching Strategies.</u> 3rd Ed., © 1990.

Right Hemispheric Functions

- LITERAL

- DEDUCTIVE

- CONCRETE

- DIVERGENT

- HOLISTIC

Curriculum Alignment

- AIMS

- OBJECTIVES

- CONTENT

- ASSIGNMENTS

- INSTRUCTION

- TESTS

Models of Lesson Organization

- TASK ANALYSIS

- CONCEPT ANALYSIS

- ADVANCE ORGANIZER

- DIAGNOSTIC PRESCRIPTIVE

Task Analysis

- SEQUENCE INTERMEDIATE AND TERMINAL STEPS

- SELECT OBJECTIVES

- IDENTIFY DEPENDENT AND INDEPENDENT SEQUENCES

- ORDER SEQUENCES LOGICLY

- TEACH

- REVISE

3-2 Orlich et al., Teaching Strategies. 3rd Ed., © 1990.

Concept Analysis

- IDENTIFY CONCEPT

- DEFINE CONCEPT

- GIVE CONCEPT
  CHARACTERISTICS

- GIVE CONCEPT EXAMPLES

3-3 Orlich et al., <u>Teaching Strategies</u>, 3rd Ed., © 1990.

Advance Organizer

- BEGIN WITH ADVANCE ORGANIZER

- PROGRESSIVE DIFFERENTIATION

- INTEGRATION RECONCILIATION

Diagnostic Prescriptive

- TEACH

- OBSERVE

- DIAGNOSE

- PRESCRIBE

- EVALUATE

- CONTINUE

Cognitive Taxonomy

- KNOWLEDGE

- COMPREHENSION

- APPLICATION

- ANALYSIS

- SYNTHESIS

- EVALUATION

4-1 Orlich et al., <u>Teaching Strategies,</u> 3rd Ed., © 1990.

Knowledge

- RECALLING FACTS, TERMS OR DEFINITIONS

- KNOWING A RULE

- CONVENTIONS

Comprehension

- INTERPRETATION

- TRANSLATION

- EXAMPLES

- DEFINITION

Application

- USING INFORMATION TO SOLVE PROBLEMS

Analysis

- ISSUES

- IMPLICATIONS

- MOTIVES

Synthesis

- RECOMBINING PARTS CREATIVELY

- UNIQUE COMMUNICATION

- SET OF OPERATIONS

- CREATION OF ABSTRACT RELATIONS

Evaluation

- MAKE DECISIONS

- SUBSTANTIATE DECISIONS

- ESTABLISH CRITERIA

- USE CRITERIA

- SUPPORT OR DISPUTE

Affective Domain

- RECEIVING

- RESPONDING

- VALUING

- ORGANIZATION

- CHARACTERIZATION BY A VALUE OR VALUE COMPLEX

Jewett and Mullan's Taxonomy

- GENERIC MOVEMENT: PERCEIVING AND PATTERNING

- ORDINATIVE MOVEMENT: ADAPTING AND REFINING

- CREATIVE MOVEMENT: IMPROVISING AND COMPOSING

Lesson Planning Cycle

- PRE-LESSON PREPARATION

- LESSON PLANNING AND
  IMPLEMENTATION

- POST-LESSON ACTIVITIES

Lesson Implementation

- UNIT PLANNING

- INSTRUCTIONAL GOALS

- PERFORMANCE OBJECTIVES

- RATIONALE

- CONTENT

Lesson Implementation

- INSTRUCTIONAL PROCEDURES

- EVALUATION PROCEDURES

- MATERIALS AND AIDS

- NOTES AND COMMENTS

- FOLLOW - UP

Instructional Procedures

- LEARNER OBJECTIVES

- FOCUSING EVENT

- TEACHING PROCEDURES

- FORMATIVE CHECK

- STUDENT PARTICIPATION

- CLOSURE

Teacher Effectiveness

- WELL ORGANIZED PROCEDURES

- STRESS STUDENT COMPREHENSION

- BE MORE DIRECT THAN IMPLICIT

Rosenshine's Effective Teachers

- REVIEW DAILY

- INTRODUCE NEW CONTENT

- PRACTICE NEW MATERIAL

- IMMEDIATE FEEDBACK

- INDEPENDENT PRACTICE

- REVIEW WEEKLY AND MONTHLY

5-6 Orlich et al., Teaching Strategies. 3rd Ed., © 1990.

ITIP Model

- SELECT OBJECTIVE

- MOTIVATE INSTRUCTION

- STATE OBJECTIVE

- TEACH MAIN CONCEPTS

- CHECK UNDERSTANDING

- GUIDED PRACTICE

- INDEPENDENT PRACTICE

5-7 Orlich et al., Teaching Strategies, 3rd Ed., © 1990.

Direct Instruction

- DELIVER TO ENTIRE CLASS

- FOCUSES ATTENTION

- MAKES MOST OF INSTRUCTIONAL TIME

- IMMEDIATE FEEDBACK

- ALL STUDENTS RESPOND

- TEACHER PROVIDES MOTIVATION

- TIME - ON - TASK

Weaknesses of Direct Instruction

- LITTLE INDIVIDUALIZATION

- INSTRUCT AT MEDIAN LEVEL

- RELIES ON DELIVERY CAPACITY OF TEACHER

Direct Instruction Steps

- INTRODUCTION

- DEMONSTRATION

- PRESENTATION

- GUIDED PRACTICE

- INDEPENDENT PRACTICE

5-10 Orlich et al., <u>Teaching Strategies,</u> 3rd Ed., © 1990.

Research on Questioning

- ENCOURAGE STUDENT QUESTIONS

- ADAPT QUESTIONS TO COGNITIVE LEVELS

- ENCOURAGE PARTICIPATION

- USE STATEMENTS TO PROMOTE REACTIONS

- USE VARIETY OF QUESTIONS

- SITUATION SPECIFIC

Basic Questioning Categories

- CONVERGENT

- DIVERGENT

- EVALUATIVE

Concept Mapping

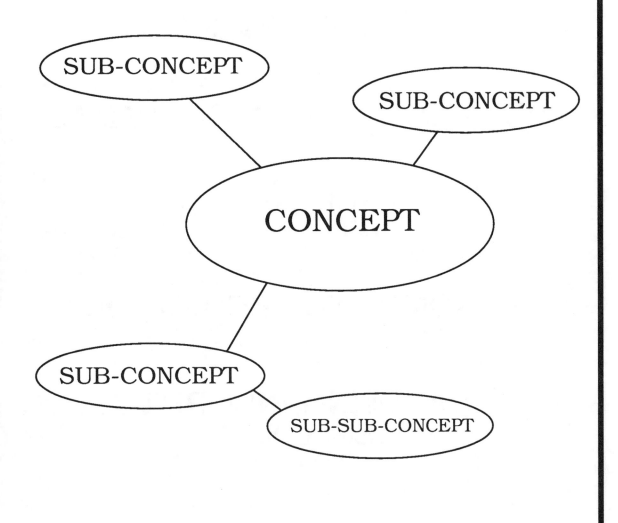

Appropriate Questioning Behavior

- BE TECHNICAL AND HUMANE

- FRAMING QUESTIONS

- PROMPTING TECHNIQUES

- HANDLING INCORRECT RESPONSES

Technical and Humane Considerations

- QUESTION POSITIVELY

- REINFORCE STUDENT LEARNING

- QUESTIONS NEVER USED AS PUNISHMENT

Wait Time 1

TEACHER STATES QUESTION

↓

WAIT TIME

↓

TEACHER CALLS ON STUDENT

↓

STUDENT RESPONDS

Wait Time 2

STUDENT RESPONSE

↓

WAIT TIME 2

↙ ↘

STUDENT ADDS
TO THE
RESPONSE

OTHER
STUDENTS
PIGGYBACK

Wait Time Rationale

- GIVES STUDENTS CHANCE TO THINK

- TEACHER SCANS FOR NON-VERBAL CUES

- ALL STUDENTS ACCOUNTABLE

Wait Time Teacher Payoffs

- LESS TEACHER TALK

- REPEAT LESS OFTEN

- FEWER QUESTIONS PER PERIOD

- MORE DIVERGENT QUESTIONS

- MORE PROBING

Wait Time Student Payoffs

- LONGER RESPONSES

- CONFIDENCE BUILDER

- FEWER NON-PARTICIPANTS

- INCREASED COMPLEXITY OF ANSWERS

- MORE STUDENT QUESTIONS

- **HIGHER STUDENT ACHIEVEMENT**

6-10 Orlich et al., <u>Teaching Strategies,</u> 3rd Ed., © 1990.

Prompting

- REINFORCE POSITIVELY

- STUDENTS EXPAND

- AVOID SARCASM

- RESTATE WITH LOWER LEVEL QUESTION

- OBSERVE NON-VERBAL CUES

Review Questions

- REINTRODUCE CONCEPTS ONE DAY LATER

- SHOW RELATIONSHIPS BETWEEN CONCEPTS

- STUDENTS EXPAND RELATIONSHIPS

- ONE WEEK LATER

- ONE MONTH LATER

Teacher Idiosyncrasies

- REPEATING QUESTIONS

- REPEATING STUDENT ANSWERS

- ANSWERING QUESTIONS

- INTERRUPTING STUDENTS

- NOT ATTENDING TO STUDENTS

- SELECTING SAME STUDENTS

6-13 Orlich et al., <u>Teaching Strategies,</u> 3rd Ed., © 1990.

Small Groups

- FOUR TO EIGHT

- COMMON TOPIC

- EXCHANGE AND EVALUATE IDEAS

- GOAL ORIENTED

- EMOTIONAL INTERACTIONS

- PROCESSES

7-1 Orlich et al., <u>Teaching Strategies,</u> 3rd Ed., © 1990.

Small Group Discussions

- IDENTIFY ISSUES

- SOLVE PROBLEMS

- EVALUATE DATA OR IDEAS

- DEMONSTRATE INDIVIDUAL STRENGTHS

- LEARN FROM EACH OTHER

- MEANINGFUL AND PERSONAL IDEAS

Classroom Atmosphere

- POSITIVE

- ACCEPT OTHER IDEAS AND VALUES

- "WE" ATTITUDE

- SUPPORT PEERS

- CONDUCIVE TO LISTENING

Critical Concepts

- INTERACTION

- PROCESS

- STRUCTURE

- ROLE

- LEADERSHIP

- GROUP COHESION

Small Group Types

- SKILL BUILDING

- TASK BUILDING

- PROBLEM - SOLVING SKILLS

Cooperative Learning

- INCREASES COGNITIVE ACHIEVEMENT

- PROMOTES AFFECTIVE ACHIEVEMENT

- STIMULATES LOWER ACHIEVERS

Cooperative Learning Processes

- VERBAL AND SOCIAL SKILLS

- SIZE AND COMPOSITION

- ACCOUNTABILITY:
INDIVIDUAL AND GROUP

- DEBRIEFING

Encouraging Small Groups

- DEVELOPING LISTENING SKILLS

- ARRANGING ENVIRONMENT

- CHARTING INTERACTIONS

- SELECTING TOPICS

- DEVELOPING LEADERSHIP

- PROVIDING POSITIVE FEEDBACK

7-8 Orlich et al., <u>Teaching Strategies,</u> 3rd Ed., © 1990.

Inquiry Models

- GUIDED INDUCTIVE

- UNGUIDED INDUCTIVE

- PROBLEM - SOLVING

- DISCOVERY LEARNING

Guided Inductive Inquiry

- SPECIFIC TO INFERENCE OR GENERALIZATION

- TEACHER CONTROLS ELEMENTS

- STUDENTS REACT TO DATA

- LIMITED SET OF GENERALIZATIONS

- STUDENTS COMMUNICATE GENERALIZATIONS

Unguided Inductive Inquiry

- SPECIFIC TO GENERALIZATION

- TEACHER CONTROLS MATERIALS

- STUDENTS QUESTION

- MEANINGFUL PATTERNS ARE GENERATED

- GENERALIZATIONS AND INFERENCES ENCOURAGED

8-3 Orlich et al., <u>Teaching Strategies,</u> 3rd Ed., © 1990.

Problem-Solving

- STUDENTS AWARE OF PROBLEM

- DEFINE PROBLEM OPERATIONALLY

- ESTABLISH LIMITS

- ESTABLISH TESTABLE HYPOTHESES

- COLLECT AND EVALUATE DATA

Problem-Solving

- ANALYZE DATA FOR MEANING

- MAKE GENERALIZATIONS

- COMMUNICATE RESULTS

- REPLICATE

- VALIDATE OR MODIFY

8-5 Orlich et al., <u>Teaching Strategies,</u> 3rd Ed., © 1990.

John Dewey's Concept of Problem

- PROBLEM IS IMPORTANT TO THE CULTURE

- PROBLEM IS RELEVANT TO STUDENTS

- PROBLEM IS RESEARCHABLE

Discovery Learning

- ABSOLUTE DISCOVERY

- RELATIVE DISCOVERY

- DISCOVERING OR LEARNING THAT . . .

- DISCOVERING OR KNOWING HOW . . .

Assumptions About Inquiry

- REQUIRES LEARNER INVOLVEMENT

- DEMANDS MORE WORK

- TAKES MORE TIME

- CONCLUSIONS ARE TENTATIVE

- METHODS OF INQUIRY CAN BE LEARNED

Critical Thought

- SYSTEMATIC

- EVALUATIVE

- BASED ON EVIDENCE

- REFLECTIVE

Critical Thinking Attitudes

- SUSPENDING JUDGEMENT

- TOLERATING AMBIGUITY

- WILLING TO QUESTION

- ACCEPTING CREDIBLE EVIDENCE

Creative Thought

- ORIGINALITY

- INTUITIVE

- QUESTIONING

- SPECULATIVE

Assumptions for Critical Thinking

- CONTENT ENHANCES THINKING

- TEACHERS DESIGN INSTRUCTION

- FEW LIMITING FACTORS

- ACCEPT DIVERGENCE

Enhancing Classroom Thinking

- SEEK RESPONSES, NOT *THE* ANSWER

- STUDENTS SUMMARIZE KEY CONCEPTS

- BRAINSTORM OFTEN

- USE SMALL GROUPS

- USE QUESTIONING TECHNIQUES

Encouraging Thinking Behaviors

- PLAN - PLAN - PLAN

- SEEK MEANING

- ASK THOUGHTFUL
  QUESTIONS

- STRESS METACOGNITION

- DISPLAY DATA

9-6 Orlich et al., <u>Teaching Strategies.</u> 3rd Ed., © 1990.

Encouraging Thinking Behaviors

- SEEK EXPLANATIONS

- RECOGNIZE CREDIBILITY

- BE PATIENT

- GRASP TEACHABLE MOMENTS

- PRACTICE - PRACTICE - PRACTICE

Three Teaching Concepts

- "FOR" THINKING

- "OF" THINKING

- "ABOUT" THINKING

Orlich et al., <u>Teaching Strategies,</u> 3rd Ed., © 1990.

Four Learning Styles

- DUNN AND DUNN: SCHOOL-BASED APPROACH

- FIELD DEPENDENCE / FIELD INDEPENDENCE

- GREGORC: STYLE DELINEATOR

- McCARTHY: 4MAT SYSTEM

Reality Therapy Principles

- FACILITATE INVOLVEMENT

- STRESS APPROPRIATENESS OF BEHAVIOR

- CREATE REALISTIC PLANS

- STUDENT IS COMMITTED

- NO EXCUSES ACCEPTED

- NO PUNISHMENT

Desist Strategy Dimensions

- LEVEL OF FORCE

LOW / MEDIUM / HIGH

- COMMUNICATION

PUBLIC - PRIVATE

Orlich, et al., Teaching Strategies. 3rd Ed., © 1990.

Desist Strategies

- GLANCE

- PROXIMITY TO STUDENTS

- SHAKE OF HEAD

- ASKING TO STOP BEHAVIOR

- TAKING OBJECTS AWAY

- PHYSICAL INTERVENTION

Behavior Modification

- PIN-POINT EXACT BEHAVIOR

- CHART BASELINE BEHAVIOR

- INTERVENE

- REVERSAL

- REINTERVENTION

Assertive Discipline

- REINFORCES POSITIVE BEHAVIOR

- NON-APPROPRIATE BEHAVIORS IDENTIFIED

- CONSEQUENCES FOR BEHAVIOR KNOWN

- PUNISHMENT

10-5 Orlich, et al., <u>Teaching Strategies.</u> 3rd Ed., © 1990.

Effective Classroom Management

- ACCENTUATE POSITIVE

- IDENTIFY APPROPRIATE BEHAVIOR

- START SMALL

- CONSISTENCY

Classroom Management

- PLAN

- ESTABLISH ROUTINES

- MAKE A GOOD START

- MONITOR ENVIRONMENT CONSISTENTLY

- PROVIDE CLEAR DIRECTIONS

- **BE FAIR**